ISLAM

A BRIEF LOOK AT FAITH & HISTORY

Revised Paperback
Edition - 2018

Hafiz Ikhlas Ansari

Light Upon Light

Light Upon Light has been established to be a positive resource for Americans about Islam in general and help American Muslims participate in the onward progress of American society.

Islam: A Brief Look at Faith and History is a unique production undertaken by Light Upon Light. We hope that this book can become the true introduction to Islam and will bring a level of trust and comfort among our large and diverse human family.

By: Hafiz Ikhlas Ansari

http://www.lightuponlight.us

© Copyright 2018
Hafiz Ikhlas Ansari, Light Upon Light, Chicago

No part of this book may be reproduced by any means, including photocopying, electronic, mechanical, recording or otherwise, without the written consent of the publisher. In specific cases, permission is granted on written request to publish or translate Light Upon Light works into other languages. P.O. Box 1477, 9114 Waukegan Road, Morton Grove, IL 60053, United States of America.

ISBN: 978-1-365-71364-4

Printed in Turkey

In the Name of God, Most Compassionate, Most Merciful.

Mā shā' Allāh, "God has willed it!"

Acknowledgments

First and foremost, I would like to thank God Almighty (may He be glorified and praised!) Who created everything, including human beings. He granted intellect, knowledge, wisdom, and freedom of choice to His special creation, humans, so we may serve Him and His creation by learning about others and ourselves. I send peace, blessings, and salutations (salawat) to the final messenger, Prophet Muhammad (may God's peace and blessings be upon him). We encourage our Muslim readers to send peace, blessings, and salutations (salawat) to him (Quran 33:56) whenever his name is mentioned. Salawat means: "May peace and blessings be upon him, his family, and his followers."

This book largely reflects the content of my formal and informal interactions and discussions about Islam and Muslims with individuals and groups. I am thankful to all individuals, my teachers, students, friends, colleagues, and neighbors, national and international organizations, mainly Madrasah Al-Arabia Tajweed ul-Qur'an, Karachi University of Pakistan, The Muslim Converts' Association of Singapore, Islamic Religious Council of Singapore, National University of Singapore, IQRA' International Educational Foundation of Chicago, Muslim Community Center of Chicago (MCC Academy and MEC Masjid), The Village of Morton Grove Interfaith Group, Niles Township Clergy Forum, The Graduate Theological Foundation of Indiana, the 2014 Summer Institute for Educators at Yale University, PIER (Programs in International Educational Resources), the Councils of Middle East Studies, African Studies, East Asian Studies, and European Studies at Yale University, and the United States Department of Education for its support and funding from Title VI National Resource Center grants, which contributed directly and/or indirectly to my growth and preparation for such conversations and dialogs.

I would like to thank Dr. Samuel Ross, Tara Ehler, Laura Krenicki, and Margaret Marcotte of PIER's 2014 Summer Institute for Educators at Yale University, Dr. Sabeel Ahmed of GainPeace, Professor Omar Muzaffar of Loyola University, Dr. John Morgan and Dr. Omer Shahin of the Graduate Theological Foundation, Drs. Abidullah and Tasneema Ghazi of IQRA International Educational Foundation, Mr. Habib Quadri, Mrs. Sadiya Barkat, and Qazi Faaizuddin Biabani of MCC Academy for their encouragement, feedback, reviews, support, and help in the publication process. I would like to thank Shabnam Mahmood and Kay at KHO Language Services for copy-editing and Saadia Malik for reviewing and editing. I would also express my special appreciation to my friends, Mr. Hüseyin Abiva and Mr. Eric Basir, for their editorial advice, comments, and contributions to the content of this book.

Finally, I am deeply grateful to my mother, brother, wife, and children (Taha, Maryam, and Yousuf) for their continuous prayers, unconditional love, and uncompromising support, without which I would not have been able to accomplish this project.

- Hafiz Ikhlas Ansari
Founder & Director
Light Upon Light
Chicago

In Memoriam

This work is dedicated to the memory of a legend and people's champion, who happened to be a proud American Muslim,
Muhammad Ali (1942–2016)
He promoted peace, justice, tolerance,
and the service to humanity.

May his soul rest in peace!

A visit to the Muhammad Ali Center
in Louisville, Kentucky is highly recommended.
www.alicenter.org

Table of Contents

Introduction: Why this Book?

In this day and age, there is perhaps no other faith on earth as misunderstood and maligned as Islam. Surprisingly, misunderstandings extend to not only those outside of this worldwide faith tradition, but also to those who claim to adhere to it.

Islam has existed since the birth of the first human (Prophet Adam, may peace and blessings be upon him). Technically speaking, the word Islam simply means submission, but its linguistic roots in Arabic also carry meanings of peace, or even safety. A Muslim is one who submits to the will of God and gains peace through following the commands of God. According to Islamic teachings, all prophets (from Adam to Noah, Abraham to Moses, and Jesus to Muhammad, may peace and blessings be upon all of them) are believed to be Muslims. However, it is understood that Islam has been around only for the last fourteen centuries. Even then, Islam has influenced, and continues to influence, many cultures around the globe, shaping histories, cultures, and civilizations. Sadly, most people receive only a two-dimensional view of Islam, which is often distorted by the brevity of media sound bites or by opinionated agendas.

To gain a truly evenhanded and thorough understanding of Islam as a fourteen-hundred-year-old religion, as well as an understanding of what's going on in the Muslim world today, would take untold hours of study and reading. Our intention with this book is to present to the reader, who has little or no familiarity with Islam, its beliefs and teachings, as well as the history of those who follow the faith. It provides the barest amount of information possible to allow the reader to look objectively at the religion of 1.6 billion people spread throughout the globe, and the tribulations that certain segments of this population currently face.

The history section of this book is meant to present, in a nutshell, the general political flow of Muslim history in the hope that the reader will better understand the present-day conflicts in the Middle East. It is not a comprehensive study, nor should it be seen as definitive. Rather it should be used as a stimulus for further detailed presentation. I hope and pray that this effort becomes a source of promoting harmony, peace, tolerance, and coexistence in our large human family through the school education system, interfaith sessions, mosque open houses, educational seminars, and individual readership.

Out of respect, we encourage Muslim readers to say: "May peace be upon him/her/them" whenever the name of a prophet or angel is mentioned. We also encourage them to say: "May God be pleased with him/her/them" whenever the name of any companion and family member of the Prophet Muhammad (may peace and blessings be upon him) is mentioned.

Islam teaches its followers that humanity is one big family originating from one father (Adam) and one mother (Hawwa/Eve), may peace and blessings be upon them both. It is also obvious from the Qur'anic injunctions that God (i.e. Allah) grouped us into nations and tribes so that we may get to know one another better:

> O mankind! We have created you from a male and a female, and made you into nations and tribes, that you may know one another. Verily, the most honorable of you with God is that (believer) who has piety. Verily, God is All-Knowing, All-Aware [Qur'an 49:13].

Islam also teaches followers that God has honored the children of Adam:

> And We have certainly honored the children of Adam and carried them on the land and sea and provided for them of the good things and preferred them over much of what We have created, with [definite] preference [Qur'an 17:70].

According to the Qur'an, different languages and skin colors are the signs of One Creator.

> And among His Signs are the creation of the heavens and the earth, and the difference of your languages and colors. Verily, in that are indeed signs for men of sound knowledge [Qur'an 30:22].

The final messenger, the Prophet Muhammad (may peace be upon him and his family), mentioned in his farewell sermon:

> All mankind is from Adam and Eve, an Arab has no superiority over a non-Arab nor a non-Arab has any superiority over an Arab; also a white has no superiority over black nor a black has any superiority over white except by piety and good deeds.

As a human family we can only learn about each other through interaction, which is also encouraged in the Qur'an:

> And argue not with the People of the Book (Jews and Christians), unless it be in a way that is better, except with such of them that do wrong, and say to them: "We believe in that which has

been revealed to us and revealed to you; our God and your God is One, and to Him we have submitted" [Qur'an 29:46].

In the spirit of sharing my faith with my fellow human beings and learning about theirs, I remained engaged in conversations and discussions (one-to-one and one-to-many) during my stay in Singapore and later in America. My interest and search led me to a course entitled "Worlds of Islam: Regional Perspectives on Unity and Diversity" in the 2014 Summer Institute for Educators at Yale University.

This one-week intensive program was sponsored by PIER (Programs in International Educational Resources) and the councils of Middle East Studies, African Studies, East Asian Studies, and European Studies at Yale University, with generous support from Title VI National Resource Center grants from the United States Department of Education. The objective of this course was to educate those in the front line (educators, primarily high school teachers) about Islam and Muslims in order to accommodate the sensitivities of their Muslim students and to respond to the concerns that students of other faiths may have about Islam and Muslims.

There were over twenty-five participants from all over America and only two were Muslims. I was amazed by the interest and enthusiasm of these educators in learning and understanding Islam and even raising questions and concerns to help their students at their locations. I was also very impressed with the course structure, the content, presenters, and their delivery. We had the opportunity during the week to learn from so many experts and scholars, namely: Dr. Joseph Lombard from Brandies University, Dr. Martin Nguyen from Fairfield University, Taha Abdul Basser from Harvard University, Richard Bulliet from Columbia University, Dr. Kristin Zahra

Sands from Sarah Lawrence College, Dr. Jamillah Karim from Spellman College, Dr. George Saliba and Haroon Moghul from Columbia University, Dr. Samuel Ross from Yale University, Dr. James Millward from Georgetown University, Dr. Abigail Balbale from University of Massachusetts, Dr. Scott Reese from Northern Arizona University, Professor Richard Eaton from University of Arizona, Dr. Joshua White from University of Virginia, and David Coolidge from Brown University.

I felt very privileged and fortunate to have been able to attend—my hat is off to everyone who was involved in organizing such a wonderful course. I wish such courses could be offered to our politicians, diplomats, officials, and the public; however, I also know certain wishes take a long time to fulfill.

At the end of the week, I returned to Chicago exhausted and overwhelmed. I was convinced that this perception of Islam and Muslims had to be shared beyond school settings.

In August 2014, I worked out a production timetable based on existing commitments. Thanks to persistence and God's grace, you can now evaluate these efforts with the production of this book.

Throughout the book we often provide references from the Qur'an and the translation of these verses can be found in the Appendix. We encourage everyone who is interested in learning the teachings of Islam to read the translation of the Qur'an and at least one biography of the Prophet Muhammad (may peace and blessings be upon him) from the Appendix.

Any error, inaccuracy, or oversight is mine alone and I ask the reader to forgive me and my team, and pray for us. We pray that God accepts this effort and in Him do we place our reliance.

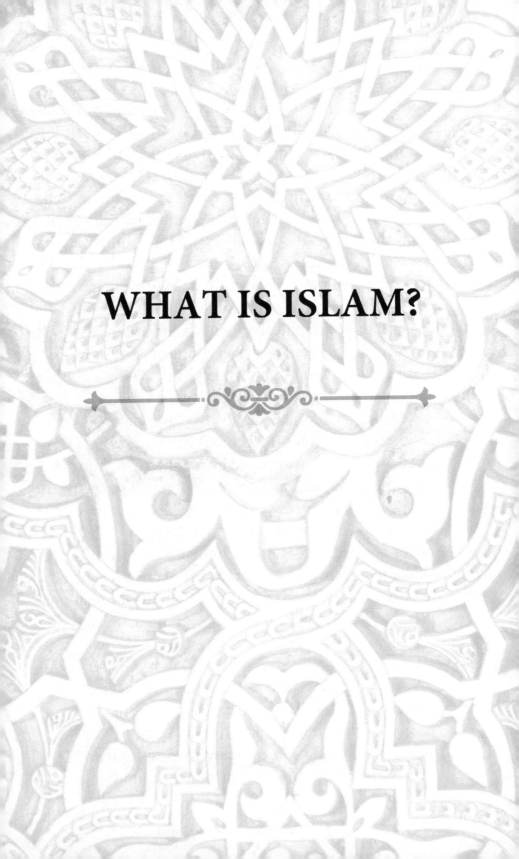

WHAT IS ISLAM?

Islam: What's in a Name?

Technically speaking, the word Islam simply means submission, but its linguistic roots in Arabic also carry meanings of peace or even safety. In the context of religion, this submission is the will of One God, the incomparable Creator of all.

One who follows Islam is called a Muslim, that is, "one who submits [to God]." A Muslim is one who believes and confesses: "There is no god but Allah and that Muhammad is the Messenger of Allah."

It is interesting to note that, unlike a great many other traditional faiths, Islam, as a religion, was not named after its founder, tribe, or geographical origin. Rather, it gains its name from a concept, a notion that everything in the universe—from small atoms to seemingly endless galaxies—all operate and function according to the will of a single Creator.

Like Judaism and Christianity that came before it, Islam is a monotheistic religion. At its core is the belief in one God, who is the same divinity worshiped by Adam, Noah, Abraham, Moses, and Jesus Christ (may peace be upon all of them). In fact, no Muslim can be considered as such unless he or she believes in all of God's prophets and messengers.

Islam is a faith that directs humankind to the way of God; it enlightens Muslims to the purpose of creation and how they are to live peaceful and fulfilling lives. In the foundational sense, there are two conditions to becoming a Muslim and following Islam:

> • Firstly, one must believe that there is One God [Qur'an 112:1–4]. This God has no partner in His absolute rule and nothing shares in His glory and lordship. Nothing can compare to God [Qur'an 42:11] and any attempt to attribute form to Him

is sheer fantasy and imagination. However, while God is beyond our mind's ability to comprehend, He is, nonetheless, closer to us than our jugular vein [Qur'an 50:16]. This belief forms the first part of the Islamic creed: "There is no god but Allah," or La ilaha il Allah.

• Secondly, one must believe that God ordained select human beings to be His prophets and messengers to humanity. These blessed individuals, who were in direct communication with the Divine, provided guidance and instruction. The first of these was Adam and the last Muhammad. This belief forms the second part of the Islamic creed: "Muhammad is the Messenger of Allah," or Muhammad ur-Rasulullah.

A Muslim is, therefore, someone who struggles to bring his or herself (or ego) in line with the will of God, and thus gain inner peace. Outwardly, a Muslim should, ideally, find tranquility as well. If Islam is followed properly and sincerely, the good manners and optimistic attitude of a believer should spread an aura of optimism and security.

Belief in One God

It has often been said that Islam is a religion of uncompromising monotheism. This is true. The belief in a single, all-knowing, and all-powerful Creator stands at the center of Islam. God (or Allah—a name which will be discussed below) is beyond all human comprehension as far as His essence is concerned, and He has no associates or partners. Thus, polytheism, man-made images of God, and ideas such as dualism or the Trinity are strictly rejected.

However, God has attributes that He mentions in His holy writ, the Qur'an, such as the All-Merciful, the Loving, the All-Knowing, the Forgiver, the Compassionate, the Absolute Just, etc. Traditional scholars have listed ninety-nine of these "Beautiful Names," although this list is by no means exhaustive.

One common misunderstanding that many non-Muslims may have of Islam is the notion that the God of Judaism and Christianity is somehow a different deity than the Allah of Islam. If it is only a matter of names, nothing could be further from the truth.

Allah is an Arabic (and hence Semitic) word that is a contraction of two words: Al means "the" and illah means "the God." What is interesting is that while the word illah can be made plural in Arabic (and hence imply polytheism), the word Allah cannot. So, Allah is the sole God, who has no partners in His divinity.

It is also worth pointing out that the word Allah is also used by non-Muslim Arabs (particularly Christians) and Allah can be found throughout Arabic Bibles. In related Semitic languages, like Hebrew and Aramaic, a similar sounding word can be found: Eloah in Hebrew and Alaha in Aramaic. In fact, we find a similar sounding word (Eli) coming from the mouth of Jesus in one of the few places in the New Testament where the original Aramaic is left intact (see Matthew 27:46). If anything, the word "God" would have been alien to early Christians (and Jews), given its root in the Indo-European Germanic languages.

Further proof that the Allah of Islam is the same God of the Bible can be shown not only in the concept of monotheism, but also in the recurring presence within the Qur'anic text of the names of many individuals that Jews and Christians would find very familiar: Adam, Noah, Abraham, Moses, David, Mary, and Jesus.

Points of Belief

As with other faith traditions, (especially those which have their roots with Abraham) Muslims have faith in things that are essentially imperceptible through the use of the five senses, and which require contemplation, prayer, and meditation to reach. Faith, in Arabic, is called Iman. Traditional scholars of Islam have selected the main items that Muslims are to have faith in and formulated these into a list; the first item—belief in One God—we have spoken about in detail above. The additional points of belief are:

Belief in Angels

Muslims believe in entities known as angels, or Mala'ika. Angels are one of the three sentient beings mentioned in the Qur'an, along with jinn and human beings. As humans are made of earth and water, and jinn of smokeless fire, angels are creatures of light. Their sole purpose is to obey God and to carry out His commands. Unlike other sentient beings, angels are in complete worship at all times. Muslims believe angels do not sin nor do they rebel against the tasks assigned to them [Qur'an 66:6]. There is also a clear hierarchy of angels, with the Archangel Gabriel at the apex. Gabriel was entrusted with delivering revelations to God's messengers and prophets, including Muhammad.

Belief in Divine Revelation and God's Messengers

Islam teaches that there has been continual communication between God and humanity since the dawn of time. Of course, a message coming from the infinite to the finite needs a channel or else it cannot be comprehended by the finite; and this channel of communication comprises divinely selected individuals. These are God's messengers.

For Muslims, Adam was the first messenger and Muhammad the last (or "Seal") [Qur'an 33:40]. Most of the names of the prophets and messengers mentioned in the Qur'an will be readily recognizable to Jews and Christians; the list includes such figures as Enoch, Noah, Abraham, Moses, David, Solomon, John the Baptist, and Jesus. While all of these prophets taught uncompromising monotheism (or Tawhid in Arabic), the legal codes that they brought differed according to time and location. A number of these men were given revelations that were, at some point, collected into a book. Those prophets given books are known as "messengers" (Rusul) in Islamic parlance. The latest (and final) of these "books" revealed by God is the Qur'an, which was given to the Prophet Muhammad through the agency of the Archangel Gabriel [Qur'an 98:2]. Although every book contains the same eternal message of monotheism, the Qur'an has superseded all previous revelations as far as the rites of worship and moral codes are concerned.

Belief in the Last Day

Like Judaism and Christianity, Islam views time as being linear, that is, having a clear beginning and end. Thus, there was a moment of creation, when God brought the universe and its creatures into existence, and there will come a moment when this creation will have run its course and come to an end through God's overriding might [Qur'an 75:6–15]. However, Islam teaches that such an event does not spell the end of humanity. At some point after the Last Day, every human being that has ever existed will be resurrected (the majority of Muslims believe this to be with a material body) to stand before the absolute justice that belongs only to an all-knowing and all-seeing God. The deeds, good and bad, will be weighed, and those found lacking will face punishment. Those who had faith, avoided sin, and carried out good works in this life will attain eternal bliss.

Belief in Good and Bad as Decreed by God

This is one point that can, at a deeper level, be somewhat complicated, however, the majority of Muslims believe in it. Since God is all-knowing, all-seeing, all-powerful, and above time, it would follow that every event is under His control, while at the level of our own limited vision and foreknowledge, we have freewill. Since we do not know what has been decreed, the freewill remains intact. In simple terms, we have a freewill to act, react (positively or negatively) and/or not react in life; however, the results of those efforts are in the control of God almighty. Therefore, we are accountable for our intentions, efforts, and actions, not the final outcome. Ultimately, God (the supreme reality) is in control of everything. Nevertheless, this reality does not release humans from the obligation to believe and perform good works. We must live our lives consciously with freewill, while resting assured that God is in control of the final outcome of our efforts, and that even unforeseen tragic events contain divine wisdom [Qur'an 57: 22].

Belief in Life after Death (Resurrection)

It is an inescapable fact that every human being must die at some point. Islam (and most other religious systems) teaches, however, that death is not the end of existence—it is merely a cessation of the life of the material body. The soul moves on to another plane of existence where one's state is determined by the level of belief and goodness that an individual had in this current life. Belief in a life beyond a physical death secures in the mind the reality that one day we will be held accountable for the life we have been given [Qur'an 83: 4–6] and knowing this should encourage us to have faith and optimism, and perform good deeds.

By and large, all Muslims, regardless of their school of thought or sect, accept these points of belief as they are clearly laid down in the Qur'an. Differences, however, may arise over their interpretation: Interpretations ranging from figurative (or mystical) to uncompromising literalism. The beliefs of smaller sects may vary from those mentioned above, usually through the addition of points. For instance, many Shi'ah Muslims include belief in a line of Imams, regarded as the rightful and divinely appointed successors of the Prophet Muhammad.

Acts of Worship

Many of us living in the West will immediately notice that Islam differs significantly from modern Christianity in that the former (like Judaism) contains a great many religious rituals and regulations. Often these regulations might be seen as being in conflict with the liberal and laissez-faire ideals that typify modern Western culture. However, to properly understand the context of the ritual worship decreed by Islam, one must understand the position of humanity in creation.

We can divide the acts of worship in Islam into two broad categories. The first category contains those that the individual owes to God; and the second contains those that the individual owes to creation. Ritual worship in Islam primarily falls into the first category, while personal communal ethics and morality fall into the second.

Human beings have been created—according to the Qur'an—for nothing else other than to worship God. Therefore, without the component of worship, humanity cannot fulfill the purpose of its existence [Qur'an 51:56].

There are many ways to worship God in Islam, such as rituals and rites that range from obligatory to voluntary. Those that are voluntary are almost endless and they are left to the discretion of the individual believer. While to an outsider it may seem extremely demanding to follow Islam, those acts of worship that are obligatory for every Muslim are, in fact, few; and they are commonly known as the "Five Pillars of Islam."

There are many reasons why they are known as such, primarily that they are the "pillars" which hold up the "structure" of one's submission to the Creator. As with the central points of faith and belief, the Five Pillars are almost unanimously accepted by all Muslims. They are (in order of importance):

The Profession of Faith (or Shahadah)

This is made with the tongue and is a verbal (and ideally internal) confirmation of the worshiper's belief in one God and in the messengership of Muhammad. The words of the Shahadah in Arabic are: Ash-hadu an la ilaha ill Allah, wa ash-hadu anna Muhammad ur-Rasulullah, which means "I bear witness that there is no deity but Allah, and I bear witness that Muhammad is the messenger of Allah." In addition to being words charged with great spiritual energy, the uttering of the

Shahadah is generally regarded as a condition of entry into Islam. Entering into Islam also means repentance of old ways of life and starting anew. It is believed that a person entering into Islam will have all their old sins forgiven and even turned into good deeds [Qur'an 25:70]. This pillar forms the core around which all the other pillars radiate and it is by far the most vital and important. The Salah forms the most important ritual worship in a Muslim's life.

The Five Daily Prayers (or Salah)

Perhaps there is no other image of Islamic worship as striking as the prayer, known as Salah in Arabic or Namaz in Persian, Urdu, and Turkish. The sight of hundreds of worshipers bowing in prostration can stir even the hardest of hearts. Salah is performed using the body, and in addition to being composed of a number of stances, such as bowing and prostration, there are a set number of cycles (or Rakat) assigned to each individual prayer. Muslims are commanded to establish the system of Salah [Qur'an 2:3].

Obligatory Salah is performed five times a day: at dawn, at noon, in the afternoon, at sunset, and at nighttime [Qur'an 17:78]. Each Salah should be performed at the right time [Qur'an 17:78]. It can be done individually, although it is highly recommended that Salah be carried out in a congregation if there are two or more Muslims. It can be performed in any clean space, although mosques are buildings constructed for congregational, as well as individual, prayer. The time of each Salah is announced by the Adhan (or Ezan), which in Muslim countries is made publicly from the minarets of mosques, while in Western countries it tends to be done within the mosque itself, so as not to disturb the peace of non-Muslim neighbors. Prior to the performance of Salah, the worshiper must make a ritual ablution of the hands, face, forearms, and feet. This ablution is called Wudu' [Qur'an 5:6].

The importance of the Salah is so great that every male and female who has reached puberty is required to perform it. Sickness and travel are no excuse for missing a single Salah (although the physical demands of the prayer can be modified). Only women who are on their monthly cycle and mothers during their postnatal period are exempt, as well as those adults suffering from mental illness.

In addition to the obligatory Salah performed five times a day, there are numerous other prayers that vary in levels of requirements. The most important (and regular) of these is the Friday Prayer (Salat al-Jum`ah) [Qur'an 62:9]. This prayer is held every Friday in lieu of the normal midday prayer. Every adult Muslim male is required to attend. During the Friday prayer, the Imam (or prayer leader) of the mosque delivers a sermon in which virtues and faith are extolled.

Fasting in Ramadan (or Sawm)

The ninth lunar month of the Islamic calendar is a month that is anticipated worldwide by Muslims, as Ramadan is a month unlike others, containing enormous spiritual treasures to be enjoyed here and in the hereafter. It is during this month that every adult Muslim male and female is obliged to fast from food, drink, and sexual activity (and smoking) from sunrise to sunset. Those who are ill, traveling, women on their monthly cycle and postnatal period are exempt from the fast, though missed days must be made up before the subsequent Ramadan or compensated for by feeding the needy [Qur'an 2:184].

Each Ramadan day begins with breakfast taken before dawn. This meal is known as Suhur. Through the whole length of the day food and drink cannot enter the mouth, and it is only at the time of the setting sun that the daily fast is broken. This meal is known as Iftar, and for those who fasted during the day, it is a sweet meal indeed! Very often, friends, family members, and neighbors are invited to share in the Iftar, thereby reinforcing the bonds of community.

It should be kept in mind that fasting is not an obligation that appeared only during the time of the Prophet Muhammad. It is a practice that has existed for millennia and which can be found in nearly every religious tradition. It is well known, for instance, that Moses, Jesus, and the Buddha fasted in order to heighten their spiritual states and commune with the Divine, and even today fasting remains a form of worship in Christianity, Judaism, Buddhism, and Hinduism.

In addition to the magnification of good deeds and worship through fasting, the month of Ramadan also contains great historical significance; it was during this month that the Glorious Qur'an was first revealed to the Prophet Muhammad as the guidance of humanity [Qur'an 2:185].

The benefits of fasting during the month of Ramadan are many. At the surface level, it is performed with the desire to obey God and His Messenger, Muhammad. Yet, fasting also sharpens awareness of one's level of piety [Qur'an 2:183]. During Ramadan, those fasting must pay particular attention to any character flaws, like hypocrisy, lying, cheating etc., because as human beings we need to be reminded and guided to the right path. In a sense, one can consider Ramadan as a training period for learning to grow closer to God through increasing acts of piety (charity, prayer, and invocations) [Qur'an 2:183] and bringing to an end the vices and passions that plague and torment one's character.

At a very basic level the act of fasting is a way to commiserate with those who suffer from hunger due to poverty or tribulation.

The fasting believer also becomes aware of the value of food and drink that God bestows upon him or her, and thus will strive to avoid wastefulness and to become more generous.

There are other pious acts that Muslims perform during Ramadan in addition to fasting from sunrise to sunset. These include a nightly congregational prayer (known as Tarawih). Before the month draws to an end, believers distribute special alms called Zakatul-Fitr to their relatives and the poor.

The end of Ramadan is celebrated with a great festival known as Eid ul-Fitr (or Bayram in some communities), during which feasting takes place [Qur'an 2:185]. This is a festival that contains a sense of accomplishment for the believers, as it marks the completion of a successful month of fasting and worship.

The Obligatory Almsgiving (or Zakah)

The fourth pillar of Islam is Zakah, a yearly almsgiving that is obligatory for every adult Muslim who meets certain financial conditions. In general, the amount of Zakah one pays is 2.5 percent of the excess wealth that one holds for a complete year. In simple terms, Zakah is calculated on the savings that one holds for one whole year and not on income. In Muslim-majority countries, Zakah is collected by government agencies, which then oversee its distribution. In countries where Muslims are minorities, this alms is customarily given to local mosques and/or Islamic organizations to distribute among the needy, orphans, and less fortunate individuals [Qur'an 9:60].

The word Zakah stems from the Arabic verb "to purify." One gives Zakah to purify the ego of selfishness and greed, and it serves as a means of atonement for one's sins. At the same time, Zakah encourages social harmony, obliging the fortunate to share their wealth with the needy.

While Zakah is obligatory, voluntary charity (called Sadaqah) is strongly encouraged. Sadaqah can be given at any time and its amount is not set—it can range from a simple encouraging word to the financing of mosques, hospitals, social welfare centers or the construction of schools.

The Pilgrimage to Mecca (or the Hajj)

The Hajj is the highly ritualized pilgrimage to the shrine of the Ka'bah, located within the confines of the Arabian city, Mecca. The Ka'bah was reconstructed by the patriarchs Abraham and his eldest son, Ishmael, centuries before the advent of the Prophet Muhammad [Qur'an 2:127]. The Ka'bah initially served as a place to worship the One God, Creator of all, but as the years rolled by it was sullied by polytheism and idolatry. When the Prophet Muhammad took control of Mecca, He re-consecrated the site to its original purpose (see Brief History of the Muslim World, page 61).

Every healthy adult Muslim must at least once in a lifetime perform the Hajj if he or she can financially afford to do so [Qur'an 3:97]. The Hajj takes place at a set time—during the month of Dhu'l-Hijjah, the twelfth and final month of the Islamic calendar.

Before the pilgrims arrive in the precincts of Mecca, they must carry out the prescribed ablutions and males don a white, seamless garment called the Ihram. With this they enter into a state of consecration and must neither quarrel, nor kill, nor commit any wrongdoing. In addition, they must abstain from sexual intercourse with their spouses [Qur'an 2:197].

Once in Mecca pilgrims walk seven times around the Ka'bah and then run between the hills Safaa and Marwah seven times in memory of Abraham's wife, Hagar, who ran between these two mounds looking for water for her son

Ishmael [Qur'an 2:158]. Pilgrims also visit Mount Arafat, which lies several miles to the east of Mecca. Here is where the Prophet Muhammad delivered his famed "Farewell Sermon." The pilgrims also throw seven pebbles at a cairn, considered to be the spot where Abraham stoned Satan, who was trying to tempt him.

With the subsequent sacrifice of a sheep, the pilgrim finishes the prescribed rites of the Hajj. Back home, the pilgrim has the right to be called Hajji, and enjoy with satisfaction the memories of having endured substantial hardships for the sake of God.

Those Muslims who do not undertake a pilgrimage celebrate the "Feast of Sacrifice," the Eid al-Adha. Every Muslim who can afford to sacrifice an animal is encouraged to do so [Qur'an 22:36–37]. At least one third of the meat from this sacrifice must be distributed to the poor and needy.

The Sources of Islamic Belief, Worship, and Morality

As we have mentioned, at the core of Islam lies the confession of faith, the Shahadah: "I bear witness that there is no deity but Allah, and I bear witness that Muhammad is the messenger of Allah." Historically, all personal and community morality, as well as state legislation, originated from these two phrases.

The Qur'an

From the first phrase "There is no deity but Allah" comes the heavenly revelation, the Qur'an. Muslims hold that the Qur'an is, verbatim, the word of God Almighty. It contains

The recitation of the text of the Qur'an is seen as a source of great blessings by devout Muslims.

no human authorship, and it was not written by the Prophet Muhammad—as many non-Muslims mistakenly believe. Even if we were to assume that this sacred scripture has no supernatural origin, historians and academics to this day cannot conclusively say who authored the book and credible theories of its origins are quite scarce!

The word Qur'an is formed from the root word that means something carefully and conscientiously read or recited. In its straightforward Arabic text, the Qur'an is roughly six hundred pages long. It is divided into 114 chapters (called Surahs), with over six thousand verses (called Ayahs). All Muslims—regardless of sect or denomination—agree on the authenticity of the Qur'an and its preservation. Of course, as with any sacred text, they can differ significantly over its interpretation [see One or Many "Islams"?].

The first verses of the Qur'an were revealed to the Prophet Muhammad by the Archangel Gabriel. The event of this first revelation took place in a mountain cave near Mecca during the month of Ramadan in the year 610 CE. Yet, it took another twenty-three years for the entire book to be revealed; ayahs came on different occasions and in different places, some of them as answers to specific questions, others with references to the trials and tribulations of previous prophets and messengers.

Even Muhammad's enemies had to acknowledge the enthralling beauty and elegance of the Qur'an. Given that poetry and oration were the preeminent art forms, enjoying the highest recognition among pre-Islamic Arabs, this divine revelation surpassed even the most brilliant of poems. Arab poets of the time accepted Muhammad's call simply upon hearing the Qur'an recited because they were convinced no human being could ever produce such verses/ayahs!

At first, individual revelations were recorded by those few who could read and write, and then presented to the public. In addition, many Muslims memorized the ayahs (which might be hard to imagine in this age of information technology!) and recited them in their daily prayers. This allowed for their preservation, until all of the ayahs were later compiled into a single book.

Once the revelation had ceased, and the entire Qur'an had been delivered, the Prophet personally determined at the behest of God the content's order of arrangement. Shortly after the passing away of the Prophet, the Qur'an's ayahs were collected from the records of those who had written them down, and the complete work was checked and confirmed by the most recognized of those who had memorized the entire revelation by heart. During the reign of the third caliph, Uthman ibn Affan, several copies were made from the original and sent to the frontiers of the rapidly expanding Muslim state. In time, further copies were made. Today, every copy of the Qur'an is identical worldwide [Qur'an 15:9]. The text has not been altered or distorted for the past 1,400 years and there are millions of individuals (known as hafiz) around the world who have memorized the divine text by heart! In fact, oral preservation was at first the main method of preservation, and this tradition continues to this day. Those who have memorized the Qur'an can trace a lineage of memorizers through the generations back to the Prophet Muhammad.

The Traditions of Prophet Muhammad

The phrase "Muhammad is the Messenger of Allah" encapsulates the second source from which Muslims take spiritual and moral guidance. The Qur'an itself stresses that for one to obey God, one must obey God's messenger [Qur'an 4:80], for as noted by the Prophet's wife, Aisha, the Prophet Muhammad was the physical embodiment of divine revelation. His character has traditionally been seen by Muslims as perfect and flawless, the ultimate paradigm of virtue, benevolence, and righteousness. God has praised the Prophet in many parts of the Qur'an for numerous qualities, of which one is his exalted character [Qur'an 68:4]. Emulating the Prophet in disposition, deeds, and character is something that every committed Muslim aspires to do [Qur'an 33:21]. In essence, the obedience of the Prophet is the key to gaining the love of God [Qur'an 3:31–32].

The sayings, acts, and deeds of the Prophet Muhammad are called the Sunnah, a term that can be defined as "habit," "tradition" or "practice." Muslim scholars began collecting accounts of the Prophet's life from his companions (and subsequent generations) in the decades and centuries following his passing. These collected accounts became known as Hadith, a word that can mean "report" or "narrative."

Unlike the Qur'an, there was no divine censure of the Hadith, and in the early centuries of Islam a number of fabricated narrations enjoyed circulation in the Muslim world. To counteract this, several Muslim scholars took it upon themselves to sift through the enormous corpus of the Hadith and develop a science of classifying these accounts of the Prophet's sayings and deeds according to degrees of authenticity. Through a systematic examination of the character of the individuals who relayed the Hadith—including those long dead—these scholars were able to stabilize the proliferation of the hallowed narrations, and eventually they were able to compose a canon of the verified authentic Hadith. This canon came to be of great importance for Sunni Muslims (who comprise the vast majority of Muslims worldwide), and second only after the Qur'an as an authoritative source for both personal and civil law. Other Muslim sects established similar procedures to compile accounts of the Prophet's sayings and deeds, although they often differ considerably as to who can be considered a reliable bearer of the Hadith. Shi'ah Muslims, for instance, tend to accept only those Hadith relayed by members of the Prophet's family.

Permissible and Forbidden

Islam is not simply an otherworldly faith that has no interest in the life we live here and now in the material world. Throughout the Qur'an we find God declaring that salvation belongs to those who both "believe and do good works;" in other words, those whose spirituality is radiated inwardly and outwardly. Therefore, there exist in Islam principles and guidelines for the way one should live one's life.

At a very basic level, two concepts basically encapsulate the entire Islamic way of life: Halal and Haram—meaning "permitted" and "prohibited" respectively. These two concepts are anchored in the Qur'an and the Sunnah, and, in the event of vagaries, the opinions of well-trained religious scholars. What constitutes Halal and Haram items and deeds are, on the whole, universally accepted by all Muslims, regardless of sect or geographic location.

As a general rule, whatever is not Haram can be considered Halal. In terms of Haram, we can classify items according to the particular sphere of one's life. The following are considered Haram items to eat or drink [Qur'an 6:145]:

- The flesh of swine and all carnivores.
- Blood in any form.
- Carrion (even of permissible animals).
- Meat offered to other deities except the One God.
- Any animal killed in any way other than the method of ritual slaughter (excluding hunting).
- Any drink or substance that intoxicates.

The following are considered Haram deeds
[Qur'an 6:151–152]:

- To worship any other deity except God.
- Murder.
- Slander and bearing false witness.
- Any sexual activity outside of marriage.
- Thievery [Qur'an 2:188].
- Usury and trading in Haram items Qur'an 3:130].
- Gambling and fortune-telling [Qur'an 5:90–91].

Islam promotes the following personal qualities:

- Justice [Qur'an 4:135] and [Qur'an 5:8].
- Equality [Qur'an 49:13].
- Liberty [Qur'an 2:256].
- Dignity of Human Beings [Qur'an 17:70].
- Humility [Qur'an 17:37].
- Hope in the Mercy of God [Qur'an 39:53–54].

It should be obvious from portions of this list that Islam emphasizes the highest and noblest of character traits, given that all such qualities and mannerisms originate from the example of the Prophet Muhammad [Qur'an 33:21].

Islamic Holidays

Compared to other religious traditions, the numbers of religiously mandated celebrations and festivals are quite small; in fact there are only two! These two holidays are known as the Eids (or Bayram). The first of these celebrations, the Eid ul-Fitr, falls on the first day following the month of Ramadan and it celebrates the end of the month-long fast [Qur'an 2:185]. The second is celebrated during the time of the Hajj, the pilgrimage to Mecca. This is the Eid ul-Adha, and this celebration is marked by a sacrifice of a goat or sheep in commemoration of the moment God halted Abraham's intended sacrifice of his eldest son, Ishmael [Qur'an 22:36–37]. Early in the morning, Muslims don their finest clothing and then gather together to perform a congregational prayer. The rest of the day is spent feasting with family, friends, and neighbors.

There are extra-scriptural holidays that Muslims have traditionally celebrated as well. The most important of such holidays is the Mawlid, the birthday of the Prophet

Muhammad. In a number of Sunni-majority countries—like Pakistan, Malaysia, Morocco, and Turkey—the Mawlid is a national holiday. In addition to the Mawlid, Sufi and Shi'ite Muslims have holidays commemorating events in the lives of their important religious leaders.

Islamophobia

Although it is hardly a new phenomenon, the term Islamophobia is a recent creation that refers to a fear of Islam and its followers, Muslims. Islamophobic perceptions are based more or less on a sharp division between "us and them," where Muslims and Islam are seen as fundamentally separate from the Western way of life. There is often a perception and depiction of the worldwide 1.6 billion Muslims as one homogeneous group, and all Muslim-majority countries as a single massive political entity. Thus, Islamophobia is a simplistic and generalized image of Islam and Muslims that has little basis in reality. It is a perception that is founded on ignorance of Islamic belief, Muslim history, and a lack of exposure to Muslims as individuals.

Since the end of World War I, serious political problems and social upheavals (often instigated by outside powers) have engulfed Muslims, partly due to the experience of Western colonialism in Muslim-majority countries. Many claiming to be Muslim have been perpetrators of violence and mayhem. Those who condemn Christianity and Western civilization for the crimes committed in the name of Christ or democracy would be labeled unreasonable. Similarly, we do not rush to condemn Islam for what is wrongfully committed in its name.

There must be a clear distinction between what a religion genuinely teaches, and the acts of individuals who may distort a religion in order to implement certain agendas or reach some material goal.

The tragic events of September 11, 2001 and the subsequent (and continued) turmoil in the Middle East, coupled with relentless negative media reports, have increased anti-Muslim sentiments in the United States. It is now common to find a number of groups and politicians making anti-Muslim statements with impunity. According to FBI statistics, hate crimes against Muslims have multiplied after September 2001, and they continue to remain extremely high.

More recently, a Pew Research Center survey undertaken in 2014 found that Americans hold more negative opinions toward Muslims than toward any other religious group. Thus, the discrimination that American Muslims face in the public sphere is a very real and tangible problem.

One or Many "Islams"?

Differences of opinion over the interpretation of any given religion are bound to arise, especially a religion that has been in existence for centuries.

Over the course of Islamic history, a number of sects and denominations have appeared and then disappeared, either through suppression or assimilation. Therefore, we will only concern ourselves with the following main groups that are still in existence to this day.

The Sunnis

By far, the largest percentage of Muslims belongs to the Sunni denomination. In fact, with the exception of Iran, Iraq, Azerbaijan, and Bahrain, every other Muslim country has a Sunni majority. Therefore, approximately 85–90 percent of the globe's Muslims are Sunni. Traditional Sunni Muslims continue to place great importance on learning and the personal imitation of the prophetic example.

Traditional Sunni Muslims continue to place great importance on learning and the personal imitation of the prophetic example.

Sunni Islam is often seen as the "default" Islam, and its core doctrines have been presented in the first section of this book. Sunni Muslims look to the Qur'an and the Sunnah (the practice of the Prophet, as recorded in the Hadith collections) as the foundation of their belief and practice. Sunni Islam is centered on scripture and ritual worship, and not on charismatic individuals (except the Prophet Muhammad). Although scholars are given great respect and deference, they are not seen as infallible human beings, and this has allowed for a wide variety of opinions in Sunni Islam on a number of ritual and legal issues—although there is a propensity towards uniformity in belief. In fact, as Sunni Islam became well established in the decades and centuries after the Prophet's death, identifiable juristic schools (called madhhabs) were formed. Today, the majority of Sunni Muslims follow these four madhhabs (Hanafi, Maliki, Shaf'ai, and Hanbali).

The Shi'ites

The Shi'ah form the largest Islamic sect after the Sunnis. They are primarily found in the Middle East, but significant Shi'ite minorities can be found in the Indian subcontinent and the Balkans. Iran is the only Muslim state to have an overwhelming Shi'ite majority (some 95 percent), and Iranian influence over Shi'ite communities worldwide is thus understandably considerable. The term Shi'ah comes from the Arabic expression Shi'at Ali, or "Partisans of Ali." The Shi'ites are thus followers of Ali ibn Abi Talib, the cousin and son-in-law of the Prophet Muhammad (the fourth rightful caliph to both Sunnis and Salafis), whom they also believe was the rightful caliph. They believe Ali and his descendants (known as the Imams) are divinely legitimized. In the centuries after the death of the Prophet, a number of movements emerged within Shi'ite Islam, which differed mainly in terms of who they saw as the rightful Imam. Two of the most notable Shi'ite factions in existence today are the "Twelvers," who form the majority of Shi'ites, and the Ismailis. While both accept the supremacy of Ali, they differ on the lineage of his successors. In terms of ritual, the Twelver Shi'ites are the closest to Sunnis; it is in belief where they diverge.

The Sufis (Tasawwuf)

Sufism (which has often been described as Islamic "mysticism" or "spirituality") cannot suitably be regarded as an Islamic sect or denomination because in terms of exoteric worship, the majority of Sufis follow Sunni Islam. Sufism is in reality a trend within Islam that focuses solely on the perfection of the self through rigorous levels of worship, reflection, and asceticism. Several centuries after it came into being, the Sufis formed themselves into brotherhoods that focused on the teachings (which are based on the Qur'an and Hadith) of certain spiritual masters, saints, or shaykhs. One of the most well known of these brotherhoods is that of the Mevlevis, the famed "Whirling Dervishes," who perform delicately choreographed ritual spinning while engrossed in the remembrance of God.

Sufi saints played an integral and important part in spreading Islam worldwide, especially in Asia and Africa. They worked at the grassroots level to take care of the needs (physical and spiritual) of the less fortunate and by serving humanity.

The Salafis/Wahhabis

The Salafi sect emerged out of the teachings of an eighteenth-century itinerant Arabian preacher named Ibn Abdul-Wahhab (from which came the term "Wahhabism"), who sought to cleanse Islam from "corruptions" it had accrued over the centuries. Ibn Abdul-Wahhab took a literalistic approach to the Qur'an and Hadith. Modern-day Salafis have come closer to those Sunnis outside of their sect. Islamic literature and causes were promoted and supported throughout the Muslim world in the decades following World War II by the oil-producing states of the Arabian Peninsula. The term "Salafism" comes from the Arabic *salaf*, meaning "predecessor" or "ancestor," and it refers to the companions of the Prophet Muhammad and the two generations succeeding them.

The Shari'ah

In recent years much has been made of the alleged threat of "Shari'ah Law" being established in the United States. Not only are such fears baseless, they are absurd—given that Muslims make up about 1 percent of the American population!

To understand the concept of Shari'ah, one must understand that Islam, like Judaism, provides regulations that not only govern how an individual believer is to conduct him or herself, but also how civil law should be enacted in the wider community [Qur'an 42:13]. Christianity is often viewed as a completely otherworldly religion, bereft of regulations that guide the worldly lives of its followers. Therefore, non-Muslim Westerners, who have enjoyed the freedoms of secularism for the last two centuries, may see Islam and its Shari'ah as controlling and constricting. Yet, there was a time in European history when Catholic and Orthodox Christianity enacted religious laws and regulations in order to ensure the smooth functioning of both church and community. These laws worked hand-in-hand with state laws to enforce moral standards and religious conformity.

The word Shari'ah actually means "path" in Arabic and the word is also used in the Qur'an [Qur'an 45:18] where it refers to religion in general. Later, the word was given the specific reference to the rulings, regulations, and laws derived from the Qur'an and the Hadith and so Islamic law came to be collectively referred to as the Shari'ah.

The Shari'ah includes ritual requirements for personal acts of worship, like ablutions, prayers, fasting, Zakah calculations, and the rites of the pilgrimage to Mecca. It also includes provisions for family law, laws on trade, economics, agriculture, and even constitutional and criminal law.

In theory, the Shari'ah is seen as sacred, although very few details of this comprehensive legal system are explicitly mentioned in the Qur'an. In reality, the vast majority of this sacred law has been developed by legal scholars over centuries. Despite the position it holds among Muslims, the Shari'ah has the ability to adapt to the times and circumstances. This, perhaps, is the great flexibility brought about by the acceptability of interpreting scripture.

For instance, some parts of the Shari'ah, such as the rights of slaves, have completely lost meaning in the modern world. Novel interpretations of the Shari'ah are also continually being fashioned, like the rules and regulations for Muslims living in non-Muslim lands, something that was quite uncommon in the pre-modern era.

Gender Roles in Islam

Islam teaches that God created both male and female [Qur'an 42:49–50] and He created both of them from one man (Adam) and one woman (Eve) [Qur'an 49:13]. According to the Qur'an, woman is not solely blamed for eating from the forbidden tree and for the fall of man [Qur'an 7:22–23].

God also assigned both male and female specific rights and obligations according to their respective natural dispositions. However, both men and woman are equal before God. The Qur'an emphasizes throughout that reward or punishment in the hereafter is not dependent on gender, and the duty to attain righteousness and exhibit virtue applies equally to both men and women [Qur'an 4:124].

Religious duties—such as prayer, fasting, charity, and pilgrimage—must be fulfilled by both sexes. However, there is some relaxation of prayer and fasting rituals for women. For example, during menstruation and the postnatal period, women are exempted from the five daily prayers and fasting during Ramadan, and fasting can instead be completed after Ramadan.

There are differences because certain biological realities exist. As mentioned above, certain obligatory religious rituals, for example, are relaxed for women during their special conditions. Also, in terms of inheritance, men are given priority since it is the man's duty to provide for his household, however, Islam guarantees women their inheritance rights. Women can earn their money through their employment or business as well. If we look at the roles that Islam assigns to husband and wife, man and woman, with an open and objective mind, they are complementary to each other [Qur'an 30:21].

Traditionally, (as it was in nearly all societies) it is the Muslim man's responsibility to provide for his family and he will stand accountable before God for the welfare of his wife and children. Just as every social unit needs structure to function smoothly, so does a family need leadership—someone who is looked upon to make final decisions. The wife's responsibility is to advise her husband and support him in making joint decisions on issues that affect the household.

The wife is the person who carries the child in her womb, gives birth, breastfeeds and instills foundational values; she has the primary responsibility for the welfare of the children. In Islam this is their most important and honored task. However, Muslim women have contributed in the past and have been contributing till today in every field of life after fulfilling their preferred roles.

The first wife of the Prophet Muhammad, Khadija, was a businesswoman. The youngest wife of the Prophet Muhammad, Aisha, was an educator. Other female companions of the Prophet Muhammad contributed medical help and support in the battlefields. The following are some exemplary and extraordinary women in Islamic history:

- Fatima Al-Fihri established Quarawiyin Mosque and (possibly) the first university in the world in the year 859 CE which is still operational in Morocco.
- Mariam Al-Ijliya Al-Astrulabi was a known tenth-century female astronomer and maker of astrolabes in Aleppo, Syria.
- Zaynab Al-Shahdah was a famous female calligrapher of the eleventh century. She was also famous for her work in Islamic Jurisprudence (Fiqh) and the Hadith. She was a brilliant and well-established teacher and was authorized to issue the certificate (Ijazah) to her students.

Islamic Dress Codes

One of the most common topics raised when it comes to gender roles is the nature of the Islamic requirements of dress, particularly for women. The dress code in Islam contains stipulations for both adult males and females. This code serves to protect one's dignity and respect. Muslims should always wear clothing that covers the body in such a way that the form of the body is not visible, so as not to draw unwanted attention. Therefore, the clothing should be neither too tight nor translucent.

Of course, the hair (or hairstyles) of women plays a very important role in their appearance and it adds to their beauty and attractiveness. For this reason, the headscarf (called hijab) is the most common manifestation of a pious Muslim woman's dress. The basis for these regulations is found in a saying of the Prophet Muhammad, where He said that only the face and hands of a believing woman should be left bare.

*Muslim dress codes (for both women and men) intend
to encourage modesty and piety [Qur'an 24:30–31].*

Women's Islamic dress codes apply only in the presence of those men with whom the woman could theoretically enter into marriage. Among the family and in female-only gatherings, a Muslim woman is not required to wear the hijab.

In reality, one finds great variation throughout the Muslim world in regards to following Islamic dress codes—especially those for women. Among conservative circles and in many Muslim lands, women additionally cover their faces with a veil called niqab. In countries with secular traditions of government it is not uncommon to find women not wearing the hijab.

Polygyny in Islam

One of the aspects of Islamic family life that many non-Muslims have difficulty with is the permissibility of polygyny. As has been stated above, Islam is a religion that covers all of the practical aspects of human life. It takes into account human nature and attempts to regulate it in a positive direction. Sexuality is a part of humanity. Islam has placed certain conditions, requirements, and restrictions on sexuality. While polygyny may seem shocking to Westerners, is such shock really justified? It is not uncommon for men living in our American society to take lovers, in addition to his wife. Not only that, but in certain segments of American society it's completely acceptable for a man to sire children with women he's not married to. So, polygyny exists in the West, however, unlike Islamic polygyny it is completely unregulated and unrestricted. In Islamic plural marriage every wife enjoys legal rights as well as the children of their marriage, and this is a much better alternative to the relationship of a man and his mistress, who has no rights.

In Islam, it is permissible for a man to marry up to four women, though this is subject to certain conditions. The ability to treat each wife with justice and financial equality is the main condition [Qur'an 4:3]. Thus, on a practical level the implementation of this will most likely be very difficult. This explains why throughout Islamic history, and to this day, the vast majority of Muslim marriages have been monogamous. Having multiple wives also depends largely on the personality of the man and the women he marries.

In traditional societies, polygamy was of particular benefit for widowed or divorced women who were without the protection and care of a husband. The norm among Muslims is monogamy. The Prophet Muhammad, who serves as an ultimate role model to Muslims, was married to his first wife for nearly twenty-five years and at the time of her death he had only ever had one wife. It was only later that he had multiple wives, the majority of whom were either widowed or divorced.

Jihad

Over and over again, concepts such as jihad and "holy war" are brought up in today's media. Actually, there is no concept of the "holy war" in Islam, even though it is often confused for jihad. The Arabic word "jihad" literally means "effort" or, more precisely, "to make an effort in the way of God." Thus, any effort made in everyday life to please God can be considered as jihad [Qur'an 29:69].

One of the highest levels of jihad is to stand up against injustice and to speak the truth about it. Fighting the whims of the ego and staying away from bad behavior are also great efforts in the way of God. Giving one's time to good causes can also be seen as a form of jihad.

It is true that jihad can also mean armed struggle and the Qur'an calls it Qital. Islam does not shy away from the fact that conflict and warfare are lamentable parts of the human condition. Such as with polygamy, it has a set of guidelines and principles that must be followed in order for it to be accepted by God, and thus called jihad. First, not every war carried out by Muslims is considered jihad. Muslim states, like any other state, go to war for many reasons, and even if parties may drape their conflict in religious terminology, it does not necessarily make it religious.

Second, a military jihad must be declared by the highest leadership of a Muslim state and have the approval of the state's body of Islamic religious scholars. Before World War I, this was the Ottoman Caliphate. While a band of guerrillas may rise up in the hills and proclaim jihad in a bid to seize control of something, it is problematic when set against traditional Islamic scholarship. Third, there are explicit rules of conduct that must be followed by those Muslim soldiers waging jihad. These codes were laid down by the Prophet Muhammad himself and they rival the Geneva Convention in their humanity and scope.

Islam is a religion that at its core emphasizes the inviolability of human life [Qur'an 5:32]. Combat or resistance can only be carried out as a last resort, and done so for the defense of one's self, home, or country. Someone who commits wanton violence cannot truly be said to be practicing his religion. Sometimes, however, violence is the instinctive reaction of an oppressed people. Terrorism and violence are not the exclusive possession of Muslims; horrific acts of terror take place in lands where few, if any, Muslims live—for example, in Mexico, the Congo, Sri Lanka, or Ireland. Sometimes violence takes place in the struggle between the haves and have-nots, between the oppressed and the oppressors, or between criminal gangs and the state. One has to differentiate and find out why people resort to terrorism, and not simply blame it on religion. In fact, much of the violence in Muslim lands that is continually featured in the nightly news is a direct result of the dividing up of the Middle East after World War I.

Nevertheless, terrorism as a means to achieve specific objectives is utterly contrary to the principles of Islam, the teachings of the Qur'an, and the example of the Prophet. Even in war, the Prophet Muhammad forbade Muslim warriors to attack non-combatants and to wantonly destroy property.

Was Islam Spread by the Sword?

The Qur'an makes it clear that "There is no compulsion in religion" [Qur'an 2:256]; therefore no one can be forced to convert to Islam. It is true—as we shall read later on in this book—that the Muslim armies who set out to conquer lands usually possessed swords; but Islam as a faith was not spread by the sword, because in many places where Muslims now live, such as in parts of China, Southeast Asia, and in many areas of Africa, we find no reports of invading Muslim armies. To say that Islam was spread by the sword, one would have to say that Western-style democracy is spread with guns, F16s, and cruise missiles, which indeed is not true. Just as Christianity was spread through the activity of missionaries who were bolstered by the military might of various Europe empires and states, Islam was mostly propagated by Muslim missionaries, merchants, and travelers. To this day, large communities of Christians can be found in Egypt, Palestine, Jordan, and Syria. Muslim tolerance throughout the centuries has ensured the survival of non-Muslim minorities. With few exceptions, nearly all Muslim-majority lands contain non-Muslim minorities.

Relations with Non-Muslims

Islam is a universal faith that teaches equality of human beings. It teaches that the differences among nations and people are part of God's design, and it is not up to us to complain about it [Qur'an 49:13]. Therefore, Islam recognizes the rights and religious freedom of non-Muslim people. In the old days, non-Muslim citizens had to pay a special tax (Jizya) in order to warrant their welfare and safety. Conversely, they did not have to pay the Zakah, which was an obligatory tax for Muslim citizens. In addition, non-Muslims were exempt from military service. What is more, Islam teaches that relations must be maintained with non-Muslim relatives to the best of one's abilities. One must still obey and respect one's parents, for instance, even if they are not Muslim [Qur'an 31:14–15].

The Prophet Muhammad forbade Muslim armies to loot or destroy churches and synagogues. The Caliph Umar did not even allow the Muslim conquerors of Jerusalem to perform their prayers in the Church of the Holy Sepulcher so as not to offend the local Christians. Jews lived side-by-side with Muslims, and the Jewish community flourished all the while they were persecuted in Christian Europe. In Muslim countries, non-Muslims generally lived in peace and prosperity; they held government posts and were not prevented from worshiping according to their customs. In contrast, Muslim minorities living in Christian lands did not enjoy the same religious tolerance, as one can see with the Inquisition and the Reconquista in Spain or, even in modern times, in the former Yugoslavia, Israel, and in some parts of India.

The Qur'an calls Jews and Christians "The People of the Book," since they received scripture through earlier prophets. Muslims are especially obliged to treat The People of the Book with respect and fairness, and not to fight with them as long as they do not start hostilities with Muslims or deride Islam. This respect and tolerance, however, is not confined to Christians and Jews. Nevertheless, they have a special status among the Muslims because of the monotheistic tradition of Abraham. Muslims carry the hope that the Christians and Jews can join them to worship the One God (the God of Abraham, Moses, Jesus and Muhammad) and to submit to His will.

The rhetoric used by violent Islamists in the current global crisis simply does not make sense if compared to the records of history and the traditional opinions of Islamic scholars. According to the Qur'an, Muslims are to interact with peoples of other faiths with tolerance and goodwill because it is ultimately God who created the great diversity of human belief [Qur'an 11:118].

Muslim Contributions To the Human Family

Islamic civilization has contributed significantly to the great advancements in every field of study including science, sociology, philosophy, and geography etc. to facilitate human life. Here are a few Muslim inventions that changed our world for the better:

1. Algebra (and more): At the foundation of our computerized world is the incredible mind of the great Muslim scientist and father of algebra known as Muhammad Ibn Musa al-Khawarizmi (780–850 CE). Al-Khuwarzimi—who lived in both Persia and Iraq—adopted the idea of the *zero* as a number. This concept opened a whole new world of mathematical possibilities and complexities. With a number system that goes from zero to nine, al-Khawarizmi developed algebra.

Initially, he used to calculate the Muslim inheritance laws. Later, he built upon the geometry of the Greeks and developed the basic ideas that many high school students can recognize today. In addition to math, he wrote a compendium on geography in which he listed the latitude and longitude of 2,400 cities around the world. This includes books about the astrolabe and sundials. For seven hundred years after his death, European mathematicians cited him in their work, referring to him as "algorismi." The modern word for a complex mathematical formula—algorithm—is derived from him. Moreover, the word "algebra" is derived from the Latinization of "al-Jabr"—a part of the title of his most famous book, *al-Kitab al-mukhtasar fi Hisab al-jabr w'al-muqabala*. This has been translated as *The Compendious Book on Calculation by Completion and Balancing*.

2. The University System: Current systems of education use a curriculum and issue certificates at graduation. This is based on the first Madrasah and the Quarawiyin Mosque, which was established in the year 859 CE by a Muslim woman named Fatima Al-Fihri in Fes, Morocco [see Gender Roles in Islam, page 34]. Another famous Islamic institution is Al-Azhar University, which was established in the year 970 CE in Cairo, Egypt. Both universities have been in operation for over one thousand years.

3. Flying: Hopping on an airplane to travel from one place to another is now the norm. It all began with the first Muslim aviator, Abbas Ibn Firnas (810–887 CE). He studied the birds to understand the principles of glider flight and constructed the first flying machine. He became the first man to fly with wings for a considerable time in Cordoba, Al-Andalus (Spain) in the year 880 CE when he was seventy years old.

4. Healthcare: Modern surgery owes a great deal to the medieval Muslim surgeon, Abu al-Qasim al-Zahrawi (936–1013 CE). He is known as the "Father of surgery." His thirty-volume medical encyclopedia was used as a standard text for medicine throughout Europe for many centuries. He served as a doctor for fifty years and pioneered many of the procedures and materials that are still used in operating rooms today. He was the first doctor to use catgut as a thread for internal stitches (catgut is a type of thread made from the natural fiber found in the walls of animal intestines).

5.   Cameras: It seems like our world is full of surveillance cameras. The modern camera is based on the rules studied, experimented with, and used in the development of a pinhole camera by a Muslim scientist named Ibn al-Haytham (966–1040 CE). He was born in Basra, Iraq during the Abbasid Dynasty. He was one of the earliest scientists in the world who laid the foundations for the scientific method. He revolutionized the approach of building conclusions through testing and observations. He wanted to understand what light is, how it works, and how humans see objects. He studied how the light enters into the eye, is focused, and projected at the back of the eye. He also studied the effect of light when it passes through different mediums like water and gases. He explained the color in the sky at twilight. He calculated the depth of the earth's atmosphere one thousand years ago. The translation of his *Book of Optics* had a significant impact on science in Europe. When his books were translated into Latin, he was referred to as "Alhazen" instead of his Arabic name. He wrote over two hundred books. However, only fifty have survived.

6.   Coffee: Around 1.6 billion cups of coffee are consumed on a daily basis around the globe; however, only a few people might be aware of the origins of this drink. Coffee originated in the highlands of Yemen during the Ottoman Caliphate in the fifteenth century.

The Muslim World

Although the traditional Muslim "heartland" is located in Southwest Asia, North Africa, and Central Asia, in the twenty-first century Muslims are to be found in nearly every country on earth. Most estimates put the number of people

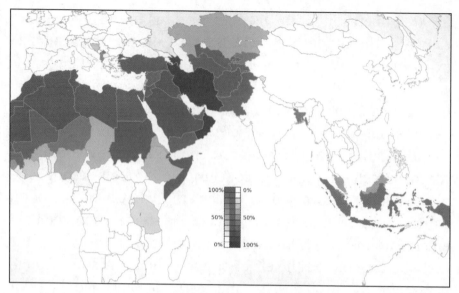

worldwide who profess Islam as their religion to be nearly 1.6 billion, roughly one quarter of the world's population.

Most people associate Islam with Arabs and the Middle East. In fact, only 20 percent of all Muslims live in the Middle East. The largest Muslim population is actually far from the deserts of Arabia—it's found in the lush tropical island nation of Indonesia! It's quite possible that half of the world's Muslims live east of the Indus River.

Muslims in the United States

Muslims today make up a relatively small percentage of the population of the United States. Given that the government does not take religion into account in its census figures, it is difficult to give any definitive calculation of the actual number of Muslims living in this country. Estimates range from a low one million to a high seven million. But even with the high estimate, Muslims make up less than 1 percent of the total population—making the fear generated by Islamophobes of a looming establishment of Shari'ah law utterly absurd.

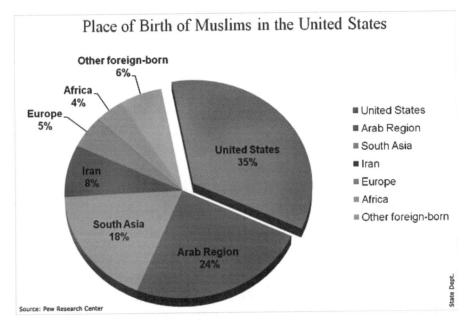

Place of Birth of Muslims in the United States

Other foreign-born 6%
Africa 4%
Europe 5%
Iran 8%
South Asia 18%
Arab Region 24%
United States 35%

- United States
- Arab Region
- South Asia
- Iran
- Europe
- Africa
- Other foreign-born

Source: Pew Research Center

State Dept.

Yet, despite such modest numbers, Muslims have been present in America throughout its long history. To simplify things, we can divide American Muslim history chronologically into four categories.

The Early Period

Although a number of scholars have purported pre-Columbus contact between Muslim West Africa and the Americas, there is no real evidence to prove this. However, it is true that, by and large, the first Muslims to come to the Americas in large numbers were from Africa, albeit in the chains of slavery. It has been estimated that 30 percent of all of the slaves taken from Africa to North America during the two centuries of transatlantic slave trade were of Muslim origin. While Christian (and Jewish) slaveholders vigorously suppressed any open practice of Islam, a few slaves were able to leave a mark on history due to their literacy, education, and considerable intellect. Yet, under such brutal, controlling, and oppressive circumstances, there was little or no hope for any of these African Muslim slaves to pass their faith on to subsequent generations.

Migrants to the New World And the Birth of African-American Islam

In the decade before the end of the nineteenth century, Muslims began to immigrate to America along with the great throngs of voyagers from Eastern and Southern Europe. The bulk of these Muslims came from Syria and Lebanon, which were then a part of the Ottoman Empire. Once in the United States, they were primarily engaged in trade and many were traveling salesmen. In fact, the first mosque built in the United States was constructed in Ross, North Dakota by Arab immigrants. A large number of Arab immigrants settled in the Detroit area as well, where they worked as low-paid laborers in Henry Ford's automobile factories.

During this time, other Muslim groups—mostly Bosnians, Indians, Turks, and Tatars—established communities of their own. Many of their centers still survive to this day in some form or another. One of the oldest Muslim organizations in Chicago was founded in 1906 by Bosnian Muslims.

It was also during this period that a number of manifestations of Islam began to develop in the African-American community. Between the 1910s and the 1930s, a number of groups were inspired by Islamic principles and a desire for independence arose. The most notable of these was the Nation of Islam (NOI), which was founded in 1930 by a mysterious figure called Master Fard Muhammad. From the start, the NOI possessed a very unorthodox ideology, an ideology that most normative Muslims would no doubt find shocking. Groups like the NOI were also strongly infused with Black Nationalism, which made them popular during the Civil Rights era of the 1960s. The NOI was involved in the historic Million Man March of 1995. A number of members of the NOI accepted Sunni Islam, such as Malcolm X (El-Hajj Malik El-Shabazz) and Muhammad Ali.

Malcolm X is perhaps one of the most influential African-American Muslims in history. He was assassinated in New York in 1965. His biography is an inspiration for all Americans and the citizens of our global village and, as someone rightfully said: "Martyrs do not always live through their ideas but through their spirit." Muhammad Ali is another proud American Muslim son who died in 2016. This work is dedicated to him because of his contributions and services to America, Muslims, and humanity.

Following the death of the NOI leader Elijah Muhammed (who was believed to be a messenger of Allah) in 1975, many of the organization's members gradually moved to various forms of Sunni Islam under the leadership of Warith Deen Mohammed (son of Elijah Muhammed). Today African-American Muslims make up a noticeable percentage of the overall American Muslim community. However, the NOI is still operational under the leadership of Minister Louis Farrakhan.

The 1950s and 1960s

The next wave of Muslim immigration came in the wake of World War II. Political refugees from communist countries eagerly sought the freedoms that America granted. During this time, a significant number of Muslims from Eastern Europe came to America, as well as Arabs and Iranians hailing from the pro-Western governments in the Middle East. These Muslims and their descendants became, over the decades, highly assimilated into the American way of life. In addition, students from many Muslim lands began arriving in America to obtain a university education. Many of these students stayed on after their graduation and eventually became American citizens.

The Present Day

By far the largest wave of Muslim immigrants was triggered by the 1965 repeal of immigration restrictions. Over the next forty-five years, Muslims from all over the world began arriving in America for a number of reasons. At first, the immigrants tended to be highly educated professionals from the Indian subcontinent and the Middle East. These people laid the foundations for many of the national Islamic organizations.

In the 1990s and 2000s, larger waves of Muslim immigrants found refuge in the United States, mostly as a result of war and famine. Significant numbers of Muslims from Africa and Southeastern Europe arrived during this time.

In addition, while conversion rates among African-Americans have noticeably slowed, there have been steady rates of conversion to Islam among America's Latino and white population in the years following 9/11.

So, as can be ascertained, the Muslim population of America hails from diverse ethnic origins. The largest percentages originate from the Indian subcontinent and the Arab world, followed by African-Americans, Bosnians, and Somalis. Muslims also tend to be urban dwellers and the heaviest concentrations of Muslims are in New York, Chicago, Los Angeles, and Houston.

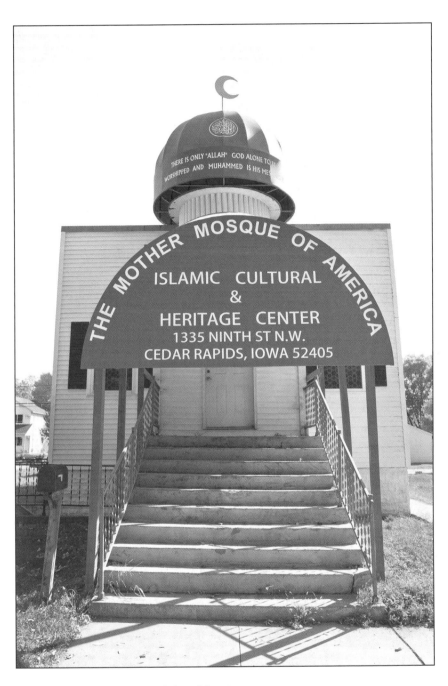

One of the oldest existing mosques
in the United States was established in 1934.

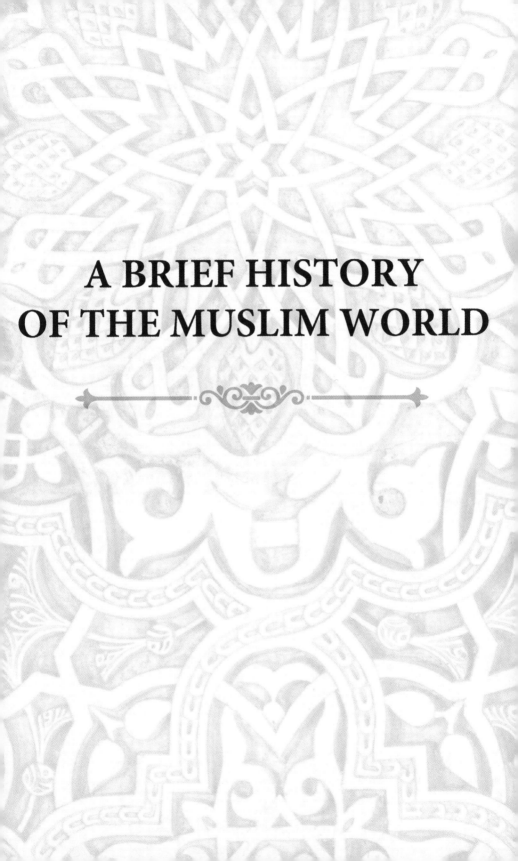

A BRIEF HISTORY
OF THE MUSLIM WORLD

Having acquainted ourselves with the basics of the Islamic faith, we will now present a brief (and somewhat one-dimensional) synopsis of the wide expanse of Muslim history. It should quickly be apparent to the reader that, more often than not, leaders and events have fallen short of the moral standards set forth by Islam. No doubt, we can see the same with the followers of other religions—even extremely devout followers— who fell far short of their faith's ideals. With reflection on the information presented, it will become clear that painting the entirety of the Muslim world with a single brush, as done today by many so-called media pundits, politicians, and activists, is naive, ludicrous, and ultimately bigoted.

It is also essential to keep in mind while reading this narration that while the tide of history ebbed and flowed, the common man and woman carried on with living their lives and building their societies and civilizations, usually unaffected by these great political forces. Farmers farmed their land, shepherds tended their flocks, architects designed their palaces and mosques, merchants traded their goods, scholars wrote their books, poets dreamed; countless millions were born, got married, raised families, and died without directly being affected by the tumultuous events mentioned here. It is also important to understand that, as difficult as it may seem to imagine, there were long periods of peace and stability throughout most of the Muslim world within its fourteen centuries of existence. For example, prior to World War I, the Middle East was one of the quietest and most politically stable places on earth.

Pre-Islamic Arabia (Pre-570 CE)

Islam originated with the arrival of the first couple (Adam and Eve) on earth and continued through all the prophets (from Adam to Noah, from Abraham to Moses, and from Jesus to Muhammad, may peace and blessings be upon all of them). However, we will discuss Islam from the birth of the Prophet Muhammad.

As a historical phenomenon, Islam emerged out of the stark environment of the Arabian Peninsula. The peninsula's center is dominated by vast and inhospitable desert areas, and it is only on its peripheries one can find fertile areas where people could permanently settle.

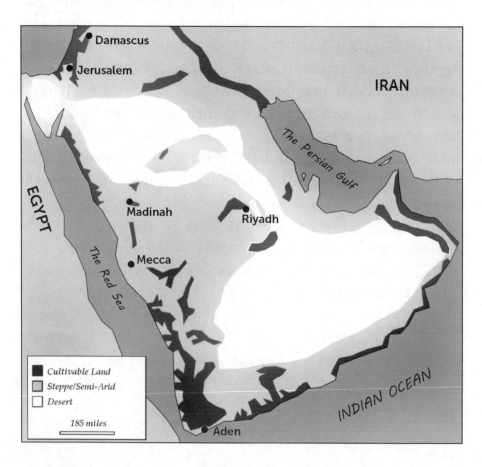

In 854 BCE an Assyrian army under King Shalmaneser III engaged a coalition of minor Syrian states at the Battle of Qarqar. The Syrians counted among their troops a contingent of one thousand camel riders under the command of an individual named "Gindibu." An Assyrian stela that memorialized the battle called these soldiers from the southern desert "Aribi" or Arabs. This is, perhaps, the oldest recorded use of the word to describe a people.

History knows well that from the third millennium BCE Semitic nomads repeatedly emerged out of the interior of Arabia to invade the Fertile Crescent, and eventually permeated throughout the relatively flat lands of Mesopotamia and Syria. The Arabian Peninsula was important for the early empires of the Middle East, given that it was a supplier of the much-needed incense used in temple worship. Incense was taken from modern-day Yemen to the north along the coast of the Red Sea. Those settlements situated along this route had the opportunity to grow prosperously; one such city was Mecca.

This trade of incense was one of the many trades that allowed for the development of a number of states in southwestern Arabia, the most notable being the Sabaeans. Their capital, Ma'rib (whose mighty ruins still remain), included a dam that was constructed as early as the ninth century BCE.

This region had become so economically important that in 25 BCE a Roman military expedition under Aelius Gallus tried to take Ma'rib on behalf of Emperor Augustus. The mission failed, with heavy losses to the invaders, who eventually withdrew to Egypt. However the famously effective dam suffered a number of failures in the century before the emergence of Islam and Ma'rib had to be permanently abandoned. This was a near apocalyptic event for the entire region.

After the collapse of Ma'rib, the fertile southwest of the peninsula fell under the control of the Ethiopian Empire. By the mid-sixth century CE, however, the Sassanid Persians gained control of the border areas of Arabia, while their mortal enemy—the Roman Empire—held firm the lands of the northwest.

A major northern Arabian state was that of the Nabataeans. From the city of Petra, the Nabataeans controlled the flatlands between the Red Sea and the Euphrates. Petra's legacy was taken over by the city of Palmyra, whose last ruler, Queen Zenobia, defeated the Romans in 275 CE.

Despite these states, the characteristics of Arab social and political structure remained tribal. There existed no political organization beyond the city-state. The many tribes formed alliances with one another and carried out blood feuds that lasted for generations. Powerful tribes often ruled ruthlessly over weaker ones and individuals without tribal connections were utterly helpless. Women were generally seen as property (like slaves), although some women from the elite class were able to amass wealth through business.

Religion in ancient Arabia centered mainly on a polytheistic cult of the celestial bodies. It was dominated by the worship of the sun and moon, and the Ka'bah of Mecca [see page 20] is said to have had a sanctuary for the god Hubal (who corresponded to Saturn). As well as Hubal, other gods and goddesses were worshiped, like the goddesses al-Uzza (who corresponded to Venus), al-Lat, and al-Manat. On the eve of the revelation of the Qur'an, large communities of Christians could be found in the southwest and far north of the Arabian Peninsula. There were also Jewish tribes found around the town of Yathrib (Madinah) and in the southwest.

Muhammad, the Messenger of God (570-632 CE)

In the year 570 CE, a baby boy was born in Arabia who would later become the recipient of a new revelation from the one and only God: Muhammad, the son of Abdullah. This child was destined to become one of the greatest and most influential figures of all time. He was born in Mecca, which is about fifty miles inland from the port of Jidda on the Red Sea. Mecca had been a center of idolatry ever since the monotheism of Abraham that was practiced there devolved into crude paganism centuries before. Here was the Ka'bah—a temple and place of pilgrimage, whose famous Black Stone formed the core of the ritual of worship. The city was dominated by an aristocratic tribe known as the Banu Quraish, which itself was divided into a hierarchy of clans.

Muhammad had a very uncertain childhood. His father Abdullah died shortly before the boy's birth. When he was six his mother Aminah took him on a journey to Madinah; on the return trip she was taken ill and passed away. The child was then taken in by his grandfather Abd al-Muttalib, the head of the clan of Banu Hashim. After two years he, too, died. From that time on, Muhammad was cared for by his paternal uncle, Abu Talib.

Early on, young Muhammad earned a living, according to tradition, as a shepherd for wealthy Meccans. Muhammad also traveled with his uncle in the trade caravans, and eventually he entered into the service of a wealthy Meccan merchant named Khadijah, whom he married not long after. Despite the considerable age difference (Khadijah being some fifteen years older) it was a marriage filled with great love and devotion. Not only was Khadijah a faithful wife, she would later become the first person to embrace Islam. The couple had several children. However, only the youngest—Fatimah—

survived her father. Fatimah would later go down in history as the wife of the Caliph Ali.

With the security of family life, Muhammad was able to find time for contemplation. His disposition was deeply religious and he often retired to a cave out in the desert hills to be alone with his thoughts. In the lunar month of Ramadan in the year 610 CE, as Muhammad meditated in the Cave of Hira, the Archangel Gabriel appeared. The angel revealed the first verses of the Qur'an, which opened with the command: "Read!" The newest and last of God's prophets should henceforth convey this divine message to his household.

The Prophet returned home in shock from the event, where he was reassured by Khadijah. He was eventually convinced through the continued (and gradual) revelation of the certainty of the mission for which God had chosen him.

The Prophet began teaching his wife, his young cousin Ali, his slave, and later his adopted son Zaid, and Abu Bakr, a fellow merchant and friend. Uthman, a member of the influential Quraishite clan of Umayyah, entered soon after into this small community of Muslims. The Prophet's teaching attracted followers from all social classes in Mecca, but primarily from the middle and lower classes. The ruling elites—who grew rich from the pagan shrine erected at the Ka'bah—met the new message of monotheism with skepticism and ultimately violent rejection. Once the message of Islam found a positive reception among more and more Meccans, those in power resorted to harassment, beatings, and torture to curb its spread. Given that Abu Talib, the Prophet's uncle, was a man of high standing among the Quraish, he shielded Muhammad from severe physical violence.

However, with the deaths in 622 CE of Khadijah and Abu Talib, the Prophet was no longer safe in Mecca. On the invitation of the nascent Muslims in the town of Yathrib (some

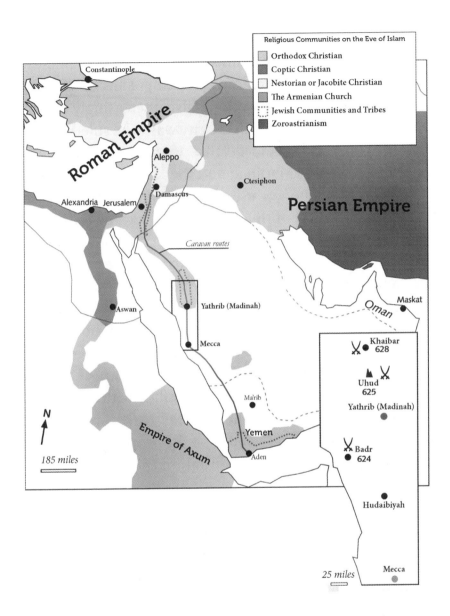

Religious Communities on the Eve of Islam

- Orthodox Christian
- Coptic Christian
- Nestorian or Jacobite Christian
- The Armenian Church
- Jewish Communities and Tribes
- Zoroastrianism

Constantinople

Roman Empire

Aleppo

Ctesiphon

Damascus

Alexandria Jerusalem

Persian Empire

Caravan routes

Aswan

Yathrib (Madinah)

Mecca

Oman

Maskat

Khaibar
628

Uhud
625

Ma'rib

Yathrib (Madinah)

Empire of Axum

Yemen

Aden

Badr
624

N

185 miles

Hudaibiyah

25 miles

Mecca

250 miles north of Mecca) the Prophet ordered the Muslims to leave Mecca. He too left Mecca in the company of his friend, Abu Bakr. This event is known as the Hijrah, or "Migration." During the rule of Caliph Umar some twenty years later, the Hijrah was taken as the starting point of the Islamic calendar.

In Yathrib (which thereafter became known as Madinah), the Prophet not only untiringly propagated his teachings, but now became a political administrator as well. He managed to settle the disputes between the feuding clans of Madinah. Many of the Qur'anic revelations also increasingly brought legislative provisions by which the city was to be ruled. A treaty of mutual cooperation and defense was signed between the three Jewish tribes of Madinah and the Muslim community.

In terms of religion, Muslim communal identity began to take shape, and many of the rituals that we know today (such as the Ramadan fast, the Friday congregational prayer etc.) came to be instituted by divine command. The first place of prayer and meeting was the courtyard of the Prophet's own home. The house consisted of a number of rooms of sun-dried brick, with the open courtyard in the center; there were also rooms of equal size for the Prophet's family members.

Meanwhile, the resentment of the pagan Meccans expanded and they fell into open conflict with the Muslim community of Madinah. When it was discovered that the pagan Meccans had confiscated all of the property of the exiled Muslims, the Prophet ordered a raid on the caravan route to Damascus, which lay a short distance to the west of Madinah. It was hoped this move would counter the financial hardships that the Meccan Muslims would now face.

Yet, the pagans would not tolerate this interruption of the flow of wealth and they sent an army of some one thousand warriors north. In Ramadan of 624 AH, the Muslims won a victory over a much superior Meccan force at the Battle of Badr. The pagan Meccans regrouped, however, and returned a year later to inflict a marginal defeat on the Muslims at the Battle of Uhud. During the course of the clash the Prophet himself was wounded and a number of his companions were martyred. The setback was temporary, as the armed forces of Mecca did not follow up their victory.

The Muslims successfully defended Madinah against a siege by the superior pagan force in 5 AH. This prolonged campaign is known as the Battle of the Ditch, from the fact that the Muslims dug large trenches in front of the unprotected entrances to the city. There is a story to the effect that this idea was suggested by a companion of the Prophet who was of Persian origin. The failure of this siege effectively broke the military power of the polytheists.

During the conflict with pagan Mecca the relationship between Madinah's three Jewish tribes and the Muslims rapidly deteriorated. Rather than side with their fellow monotheists, the Jewish chiefs entered into secret negotiations with the pagans. Two of these tribes were expelled from Madinah as punishment for their treason, and the third was dealt with according to the Torah's penalty for treason.

The clashes with surrounding pagan tribes continued throughout the seventh year after the Hijrah. That year, however, under the terms of a truce negotiated with the Meccans, the Prophet was able to make the pilgrimage to the Ka'bah with a large number of Muslims. This was the first time he had returned home since the migration to Madinah.

In the eighth year, the truce with pagan Mecca was breached because of an attack carried out against a Muslim camp. The Prophet gathered a force of ten thousand men and retaliated by marching on his native city. In a magnanimous act of clemency, the Muslims took possession of the city without bloodshed. They did, however, destroy all of the pagan idols that defiled the sacred Ka'bah. Following this, the Prophet returned to Madinah.

After Mecca was conquered by the Muslims, deputations were sent to the many tribes of the Arabian Peninsula, who for the most part accepted Islam as their faith and the Prophet as their political head. Letters were also sent to the heads of the empires and states that surrounded Arabia, calling them to embrace the new monotheistic dispensation.

The following year, the Prophet made the pilgrimage to Mecca with great solemnity. He was now over sixty years of age and the demanding life of his prophethood had taken its toll; he fell ill during the return journey. The Prophet returned to Madinah, but the illness had not subsided. During his bed rest, he authorized a military expedition against the territory that is now Jordan, in order to strike at hostile Arab tribes and their Roman supporters.

In 632 CE the Prophet of Allah passed from this world. At first there was dismay among Muslims, but when Abu Bakr heard this, he announced to the gathering crowd, "Whosoever worships Muhammad, let him know that he has passed! But to those who worship Allah, let it be known that Allah does not die!" The aging Abu Bakr, who had been one of the first to embrace Islam, became the first caliph, or successor to the Prophet.

This, in a nutshell, is the life of Muhammad, the Messenger of God. The religion that he taught and the book that he presented would affect the course of world history for the next fourteen hundred years.

The Four "Rightly Guided Caliphs" (632–661 CE)

For thousands of years an invisible cultural border intersected the Middle East. It separated the fertile plains of Mesopotamia from the barren eastern highlands of Persia. Again and again throughout history the tribes and people that poured over these mountains came into conflict with the settled people of the plains. Such conflict existed on the eve of Islam, as Rome and Persia battled for supremacy in the Fertile Crescent.

During the lifetime of the Prophet, the clash between Zoroastrian Persia and Christian Rome took on previously unknown proportions. The Persians succeeded in bringing large parts of Syria, Egypt, and Asia Minor under their control between 610 and 616 CE. However, a huge Roman counter-offensive (mentioned in the Qur'an) pushed the Persians out and inflicted such a blow that the foundations of the Persian Empire were undermined [Qur'an 30:2–4]. Evidently, this was a Pyrrhic victory for Rome, as the empire was financially and militarily bled dry by the years of war. The once-effective and powerful Roman army had lost its best fighters. At this point it consisted mostly of inexperienced European and North African mercenaries, who, as members of an occupying force, terrorized and oppressed local populations throughout Iraq, Syria, and Egypt. The defeated Persians disintegrated into routine civil

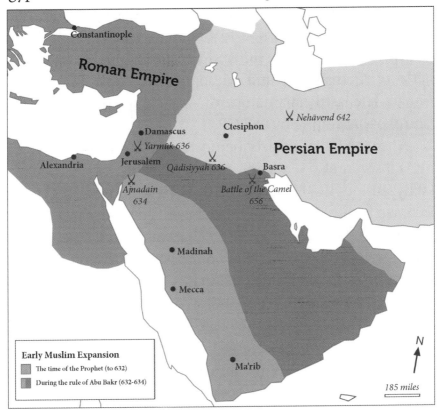

war. Thus, when the battle-hardened, but poorly-equipped, Muslim armies surged out of the Arabian Peninsula in the years following the Prophet's passing, Rome and Persia stood little chance of resisting.

Given that the Prophet made no stipulation related to his successor, the companion Abu Bakr was chosen by consensus to lead the community as caliph, or "deputy." During Abu Bakr's caliphate, Islam spread throughout the entire Arabian Peninsula. His rule, however, was a mere two years. Upon his deathbed, he appointed another long-standing companion of the Prophet to assume the position of caliph: Umar ibn al-Khattab. Islamic tradition speaks of Umar as being a humble yet strict man.

The Caliph Umar (who ruled from 634–644 CE) added significant territory to the blossoming Muslim state. In 635 CE the important Roman city of Damascus capitulated to the Muslims, and Palestine entered the caliph's control in 638 CE after Jerusalem fell due to the victory at Yarmuk. In the northeast, the Persians suffered a catastrophic defeat at the Battle of Qadisiyyah, and Mesopotamia came under Arab control. The last Persian emperor, Yezdegerd III, lost complete control of his empire by 642 CE.

After the fall of the frontier fortress of Pelusium in 640 CE, the Arabs were also venturing into the Nile Valley. That same year, the Byzantines lost a decisive battle at Heliopolis and Egypt was occupied by the Arabs. The majority of Christian Egypt (which belonged to the Monophysite sect that was branded heretical by Rome) welcomed the Muslim conquest as liberators from the oppression of the Orthodox Church.

Camp towns were set up in the conquered territories, from which the warrior aristocracy ruled. The most important were Kufa and Basra, which emerged in Iraq, and al-Fustat, on the edge of what was to become Cairo. For quite some time the Arabs remained dependent on the cooperation of the local elites, who were, for the most part, Christians. After all, they were primarily nomads carrying primitive political and administrative skills unfit for running vast holdings. The newly conquered territories were highly developed urban-artisan or peasant civilizations. Yet, in a relatively short time the Arabs were able to assimilate much of their conquered subjects' culture and proficiency.

In 644 CE Umar was assassinated by a Persian servant from Kufa. A council of elders selected Uthman to be the next caliph. Uthman was the member of the clan of Banu Umayyah, which had lost its predominant position among the Quraish with the victory of Islam. Under Uthman's guidance the Qur'an was codified into a bound standard edition by 653 CE. On the military front, the Arab armies moved further westward, occupying Tripoli in 647 CE. A newly built fleet inflicted such a heavy defeat on the Byzantine navy in 655 CE that the Emperor Constans II hastily moved his capital from Constantinople to Syracuse in Sicily.

However, a coup shook the caliphate in 656 CE when disgruntled Arab warriors from Egypt killed Uthman in Medinah as he read the Qur'an in his home. A battle for his succession paralyzed the empire. The popular appointment of Ali as caliph split the Muslim community. As the son-in-law (and first cousin) of the Prophet, and the father of Hasan and Husain (the only male descendants of the Prophet), Ali enjoyed a high standing. However, many turned against him, especially the members of the clan from which Uthman hailed: the Bani Umayyah, the "Umayyads." While Ali was able to contend with an uprising in southern Iraq that was led by the favorite wife of the Prophet, the rebellious governor of Syria, the Umayyad chief Mu'awiyah, proved to be a far more determined opponent.

In 657 CE the armies of Ali and Mu'awiyah clashed along the Euphrates at the Battle of Siffin. While Ali's troops initially maintained the upper hand, the caliph opened negotiations with Mu'awiyah and made concessions to him. This sparked resentment among many serving in Ali's ranks and a sizeable group split away from him. This group was known as the Kharijites, and in their uncompromising religious fanaticism they declared all who were not with them, including both Ali and Mu'awiyah, to be infidels. Ali became involved in fighting the mutinous Kharijites and he was assassinated by one of their members in 661 CE in the mosque of Kufa.

The Rule of the Umayyad Clan (661–750 CE)

Having secured his claim to be the ruler of the rapidly expanding Muslim state, Mu'awiyah moved its capital from Madinah to Damascus, which was a far more cosmopolitan city, inhabited mainly by Christians. Subsequently, the center of Muslim power moved more and more from the Arabian Peninsula to Syria, Iraq and, later, Egypt. In the following years, new military successes were achieved: in the east Kabul fell to the Arabs in 664 CE, and in 674 CE they conquered Samarkand. Far to the west, Kairouan (in today's

Tunisia) was founded in 670 CE as a purely Arab town. However, the indigenous Berber tribes, supported by the Byzantines, proved to be a source of fierce resistance in the region. Also, in 669 CE the first attempt to take the imperial city of Constantinople failed, not in the least because the defenders used "Greek fire," a napalm-like substance

that effectively destroyed and damaged the Muslim navy. This left the Romans (or Byzantines) masters of the Mediterranean Sea routes, while the Arabs dominated the overland trade routes throughout the Middle East and Central Asia; therefore they controlled the ancient trade routes between Europe and the Far East.

When Mu'awiyah died in 680 CE, civil conflict again erupted between Muslims. The Iraqi garrisons (who had supported Ali in the first civil war) turned against Mu'awiyah's son Yazid I, who inherited the office of caliph. In their view, Husain, the son of the Caliph Ali (and grandson of the Prophet), deserved the honor to lead the Muslim community. Husain placed himself at the head of this doomed uprising, and he fell in 680 CE at the Battle of Karbala fighting a huge Umayyad force. This can be seen as a significant event, for now the followers of Ali and Husain grouped themselves under the name Shi'atu 'Ali, or "Partisans of Ali," and Islam came to be clearly divided henceforth into Sunnis and Shiites [see One Islam or Many "Islams"?].

The unity of the young empire became vulnerable, especially when another anti-Umayyad uprising broke out in Mecca; during its suppression even the Ka'bah came under fire. After a long struggle, the Umayyads only managed to reunify the caliphate by 691 CE. It was during this time that the Umayyads constructed in Jerusalem a magnificent mosque on the spot where the Prophet had ascended into heaven during the "Night Journey," or the 'Isra' wal Mi'raj. However, they suffered a serious impediment in their North African campaign. In 693 CE, with the help of the Byzantine fleet, the Berber tribes crushed an Arab army in modern-day Libya. It took nearly a decade to rectify this setback; and when it was, the Umayyads pressed onward to Morocco.

Caliph Abd al-Malik (685–705 CE), a ruler with an energetic personality, consolidated the empire through the implementation of profound reforms. The administrative apparatus of the Umayyad state was Arabized, with Christian and Persian officials forced out of office. Arabic (rather than Greek, Persian, or even Aramaic) became the administrative language and the monetary system was unified as well.

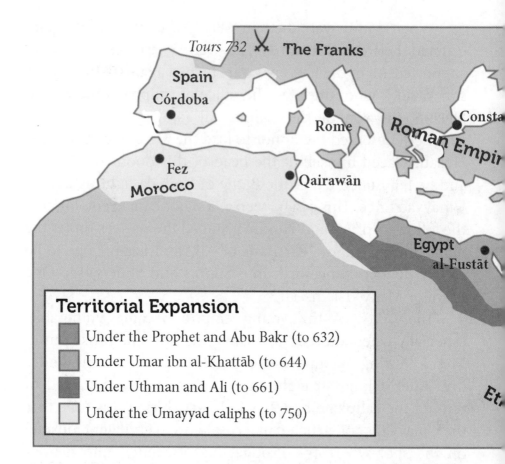

Tours 732 ✕✕ The Franks

Spain
Córdoba ●

Rome ●

Roman Empir

Consta ●

Fez ●
Morocco

Qairawān ●

Egypt ●
al-Fustāt

Territorial Expansion

Under the Prophet and Abu Bakr (to 632)
Under Umar ibn al-Khattāb (to 644)
Under Uthman and Ali (to 661)
Under the Umayyad caliphs (to 750)

Et.

As regards to its geographical expansion, the Umayyad Caliphate reached its zenith during this time. In the west, after the Battle of Guadalete in 712 CE, almost the entire Iberian Peninsula fell under Muslim rule; Islam had arrived in Europe. In the east, the Arabs reached the Fergana Valley in Central Asia and the northern side of the Caucasus Mountains. A second siege of Constantinople again failed in 717 CE.

However, civil unrest continually threatened Umayyad rule. Caliph Umar ibn Abd al Aziz (717–720 CE), a man viewed by Muslims as one of the pious Umayyad rulers, halted official discrimination against the steadily growing number of non-Arab Muslims, who had been until that time heavily taxed regardless of their conversion to Islam. He also attempted to alleviate the tensions between Sunnis and Shiites.

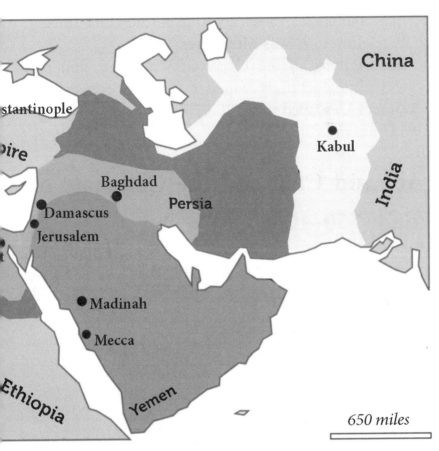

Under Umar's brother and successor, Yazid II (720–724), unrest flared up in nearly all parts of the empire: in Central Asia, North Africa, and along the Nile. In 732 CE a Muslim invasion of France was driven back by Charles Martel at the Battle of Tours. This may have been important for the future of Christian Europe, but it was irrelevant to the situation of the caliphate at the time.

In 747 CE a revolt broke out in Central Asia that the Umayyads could not contain. A rebel by the name of Abu Muslim (who was possibly Persian) led a multi-ethnic army to seize Persia and Iraq from the Umayyads. In 749 CE the rebellion proclaimed a chief of the Abbasid clan, Abu'l Abbas as-Saffah, as caliph. This clan traced its origins back to the

Prophet's paternal uncle, Abbas, and thus it sought legitimacy through its relation to Allah's Messenger.

The Arab empire of the Umayyads collapsed, and the dynasty was almost entirely wiped out. Only one prince, Abdur-Rahman I, escaped to the Iberian Peninsula, where he continued Umayyad rule.

The Abbasid Clan and the Caliphate of Baghdad (750–1258 CE)

The initial foreign policy of the Abbasid Caliphate was almost exclusively on the defensive. Iberia was lost to the rival Umayyads, and North Africa eluded central authority. When the Abbasids eventually executed their own loyal commander, Abu Muslim, widespread insurgence broke out in Persian

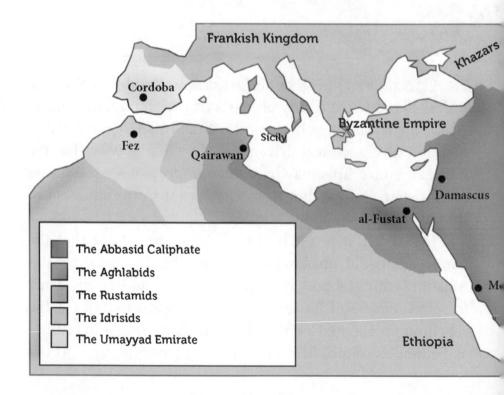

lands, which was suppressed. Lebanese Christians likewise rebelled with support from the Byzantine Empire.

Efforts were made in Upper Egypt and in northern Persia for greater autonomy. However, all of this commotion did not place the caliphate in question. Even the Iberian Umayyads set aside their claim to the caliphate and simply adopted the title of amir, roughly translated as "commander-in-chief." For the most part, the Abbasids left the periphery of the Muslim world to its own devices as they focused on the Middle East. Caliph Al-Mansur moved the caliphate's capital from Damascus (which had been the stronghold of the Umayyads) to Baghdad in Iraq, where he built an entirely new administrative seat in 762–63 CE.

The City of Peace: (Madīnat us-Salām)

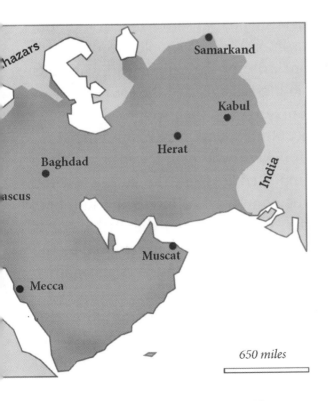

Baghdad was initially designed with a circular layout, which had a diameter of a mile and a half. In the center was the caliph's palace with its mosque and barracks. Encircling the center of governmental buildings were residential and commercial buildings. Four roads led from the center point to four fortified gates. A double wall surrounded the city and fortifications separated four great quarters from each other. The main roads into the circular city were closed at night. Outside of the city walls huddled throngs of merchants, peasants, and soldiers of fortune. In time, homes and shops were built and the city grew in size.

Baghdad was an expression of the new and highly centralized form of government instituted by the Abbasids. Unlike the Umayyads, who relied heavily on the old Arab tribal structure to rule, the Abbasids were absolute monarchs, much more in the fashion of the Roman and Persian emperors.

The flowering of the caliphate at Baghdad is epitomized (at least in the West) with the legendary Caliph Harun al-Rashid (786–809 CE). Yet, the reality of his reign was certainly less glamorous than its portrayal in "A Thousand and One Nights." Harun al-Rashid was unable to break Byzantine naval supremacy in the Mediterranean, and thus control over North Africa was completely lost to smaller Muslim states. In addition, the tax system began to crumble due to a simple lack of control of the population. The majority of the caliphate's inhabitants were peasant farmers who increasingly fled the countryside or were killed in the many uprisings and their suppressions.

More and more concentrated land ownership came into the hands of powerful elites, who paid fewer taxes. More and more slaves were imported to work the land; even the Abbasid army came to be composed of increasing numbers of slaves and mercenaries, primarily from the Turkic tribes of Central Asia. These mercenaries came to be favored by the caliph over the long-established Arabic and Persian nobility. This would later on prove to be a fatal mistake.

In striking contrast to this economic and administrative crisis was the flourishing of art and science, which continued under Caliph Al-Ma'mun, the son of Harun al-Rashid. He patronized poets, philosophers, and scientists with state funds. Legendary is the translation of classical Greek works into Arabic—at a time when Europe sat in the Dark Ages. Muslim scholars, it can justly be said, preserved the ancient heritage of the West. Muslim mathematicians and astronomers influenced the Europeans with their insights into Indian science, and with the transference of this knowledge came the unknown number zero.

Muslim merchants plied the sea routes of the Indian Ocean southwards along the East African coast and eastwards all the way to the Moluccas. With them came the teachings of the Prophet.

As the size of Baghdad increased to that of a mega-city, a new city, Samarra, was built in 836 CE. This location served as the Abbasid capital for sixty years before being moved back to Baghdad. One of the more remarkable structures erected in Samarra was the Great Mosque, which (including its expansive courtyard) could accommodate one hundred thousand worshippers.

The Center Cannot Hold

During this period, the meddling of the Turkic slave-soldiers in the government increased, and they bullied the Abbasid caliphs into extending their own power and influence. Any caliph (or courtier) who dared to oppose them was simply murdered and replaced with a more compliant nominee. New African mercenaries were, in vain, brought in as a military counterweight to the Turks.

The growing weakness of the central power led to the flourishing of Muslim states on the periphery of the empire. On the Iberian Peninsula the once-ascendant Umayyads had long been charting a course of their own, far removed from

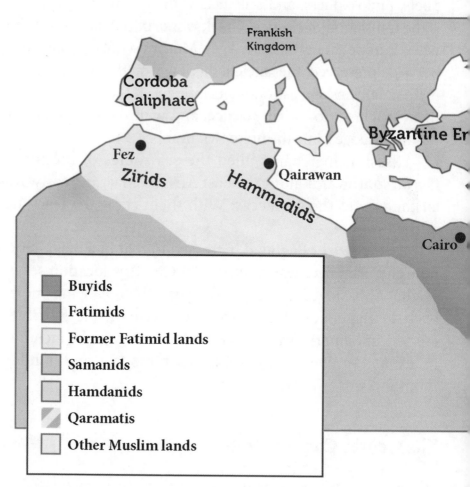

Baghdad. The Idrisid Dynasty held sway over Morocco from their capital of Fez, while the Aghlabids (descendants of an Abbasid governor) created their own state that stretched from Algeria to Libya. With an accomplished navy, the Aghlabids succeeded in taking Sicily from the Byzantines after a nearly seven-decade-long campaign. As a major Mediterranean maritime power, the Aghlabids amassed the riches with which to execute magnificent building projects, especially in Kairouan and Tunis.

In 868 CE, Egypt broke away from the Abbasid state after its Turkic governor, Ahmad ibn Tulun, declared its de facto

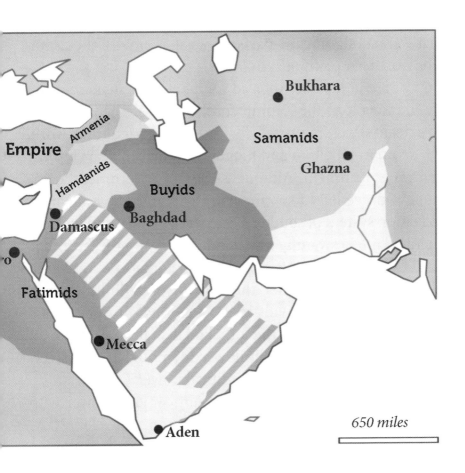

650 miles

independence. Although Tulunids were hated by the majority of Egyptians (who were Arabs and Copts) as ethnically alien rulers, they advanced the country with a well thought out irrigation policy and they promoted trade and industry.

Independence movements also took hold in the East. Among others, the Samanid Dynasty (which had deep roots in the Persian nobility) came into being in 819 CE and, with the city of Bukhara as its main center, lasted for some 180 years. In 999 CE the last of the Samanid rulers was overthrown by Turkic mercenaries, who established in its ruins the Ghaznavid Empire. Though centered in what is now Afghanistan, the

Ghaznavids came to rule, over the course of two centuries, eastern Persia, significant parts of what is now Uzbekistan, and the northern plain of India.

In its core lands, the Abbasid Caliphate was shaken in 868 CE by the Revolt of the Zanj in southern Iraq. The Zanj were East African slaves imported for grueling agricultural work. They rose up in rebellion and fought for fourteen years against the central government. Although Abbasid government forces eventually succeeded in suppressing the revolt, the millennia-old irrigation system of southern Iraq was in ruins, and the land degenerated into a swampy wasteland. The economic fate of the Abbasid Caliphate was thus sealed long before its political end.

The caliph came under the control of a Shiite Persian dynasty known as the Buyids in 945 CE. Buyid princes ruled with the grand Persian title of Shahanshah (or "King of Kings"), while the Abbasid caliphs were demoted to exclusively religious figureheads devoid of political power.

In North Africa, a Shiite movement came to power with the Fatimid Dynasty. Their legitimacy lay in their claim they were descended from the Prophet Muhammad's daughter, Fatimah. Rising up from their base in North Africa, the Fatimids overthrew Aghlabid rule in 909 CE and by 969 CE were in control of Egypt. The city of Cairo was founded not far from the military camp of al-Fustat, and it became the center of their power; a splendid flowering of Arab-Islamic culture was thus initiated. The Al-Azhar Mosque, founded by the Fatimids in 971 CE, became one of the most important Muslim places of worship, and it later became the center of an important university that is still in operation today.

From Central Asia, a new power arose in the Muslim world: the Seljuk Turks. Staunch Sunnis, the Seljuks overthrew the Shiite Buyids and established their own hegemony over the Abbasid Caliphate. At its height, the Seljuk Empire stretched from the shores of the Aegean to the Amu Darya. It was the achievements of the Seljuks that sparked the first of two invasions that were to hit the Muslim world in the eleventh through thirteenth centuries.

Threats from East and West

During the eleventh century, Muslims were thrown on the defensive. Muslim Iberia came under pressure from the Christian Reconquista, conquests in Sicily were lost, and Byzantium still defied all attacks. In the east, massive waves of Turkish tribes began pouring into the Middle East from Central Asia. Although the Turks had embraced Islam, they threw into question the Arab domination of not only Muslim politics, but also culture, society, and religion as well. While all this was going on, the Pope in Rome realized the chance to strengthen the power of Western Christendom. Until now, it had been on the retreat before Islam. All of the sacred sites associated with early Christianity had been in Muslim hands for nearly five centuries. Now, the opportunity seemed favorable to strike back.

The Crusades (1095–1291 CE)

In November 1095 CE, the Council of Clermont was held. Ten years earlier, the Reconquista had already reached the Tagus River in Spain, placing the Muslims there on the defensive. In the east, however, Muslim power, in the shape of the Seljuks, continued to press Orthodox Christian Byzantium. In 1095 CE, its ruler, Emperor Alexius I Comnenus, turned to his Catholic brothers in the West for assistance against the Turkish onslaught. Pope Urban II responded favorably, perhaps seeing this as a chance to assert the power of the Catholic Church over the Orthodox East. A call was issued at the aforesaid Council to fight against the "barbarians," i.e. Muslims. As a reward, the Church assured the forgiveness of sins and eternal life.

It was mainly French and German knights who headed the call of what was to be the First Crusade, although there came many ordinary people from among the urban class and the peasantry. The Christian army was headed by Duke Godfrey of Bouillon, a rather level-headed nobleman. A so-called "Peasants' Crusade" led by a hermit gathered the lower classes of Western Europe and set out before the official Crusade. Their first target on their long march to Asia Minor was not Muslims, but the other infidels of Europe: the Jews. Jews were massacred, robbed, and abused all along the route. However, having arrived at the front in 1096 CE, the Peasants' Crusade did not survive long. It was annihilated by a Seljuk army after barely setting foot into Asia Minor.

The official Crusader army was a different story, and through their military skill they succeeded in taking the capital of the Anatolian Seljuks in May 1097 CE. The following year the Syrian cities of Edessa and Antioch fell, and from them emerged the first Crusader states.

The Fatimids in Egypt took advantage of the opportunity opened by the battling of the Seljuks and Crusaders, and occupied Jerusalem. Any further steps to the south meant that the Crusaders would have to confront Cairo in addition to the Turks. However, in June 1099 the Christian knights had reached the holy city, which was the real target of their efforts. After nearly one month's siege, the Christians stormed the city on July 15 and initiated such a slaughter of its inhabitants—Muslim and Jew, civilian and solider—that it is remembered to this day. With this, the last of the Crusader states, the Kingdom of Jerusalem was established, with Godfrey of Bouillon as its king.

The location of these small states caused them to remain unstable, and thus, further Crusades were necessary to ensure their survival. By the end of 1143 CE Edessa was lost. The overthrow of the Fatimids in 1169 CE and the establishment of a staunchly Sunni Ayyubid Dynasty in Egypt and Syria finally took care of any threat, and it would be a long time before Europeans invaders would prove a match for the Muslims. The famed Sultan Saladin (Salah ud-Din), the founder of the Ayyubid Dynasty, proved to be a skillful commander and he destroyed a Crusader army at the Battle of Hattin in 1187 CE, and then recaptured Jerusalem.

In 1202 CE a Fourth Crusade was proclaimed but it proved to be a farce. Instead of moving against Muslim enemies, it instead conquered the city of Constantinople (which was Orthodox Christian), thereby establishing the short-lived "Latin Empire." What the Muslims had for centuries been unable to do had now happened: a long-term weakening of the eastern flank of Christendom. A Fifth Crusade attempted to strike the Ayyubids in their own territory of Egypt. It managed to seize the port of Damietta in 1219 CE, but its advance inland was totally crushed.

In 1228 CE, Jerusalem again fell into Western possession, this time not by military force, but rather through negotiation. The leader of this Crusade, the cosmopolitan Emperor Frederick II (who was excommunicated by the Pope for, among other things, his pro-Islamic leanings—he spoke Arabic!) acted in conjunction with Sultan al-Kamil to ensure a degree of freedom for the city's Muslim population. However, after the Battle of Gaza in 1244 CE, the city was finally lost. Hope for Christians briefly burgeoned when the Mongols invaded from the east, destroying a number of Muslim states, but their attempt to conquer Syria was defeated in 1260 CE by the Muslim Mamluks at the Battle of Ain Jalut. After that, the remaining Crusader towns and castles fell one by one, with the last, Acre, coming under Mamluk control in 1291 CE. With that the medieval Western Christian intermezzo in the Middle East came to an end. For most Muslim chroniclers of the time, the Crusades were simply one bloody event among many and, at best, a marginal side note. In Christian Europe, however, they were particularly overrated. The Crusader states were simply short-term, pesky splinters in the constitution of the Muslim world. Their cities—Cairo and Baghdad, and

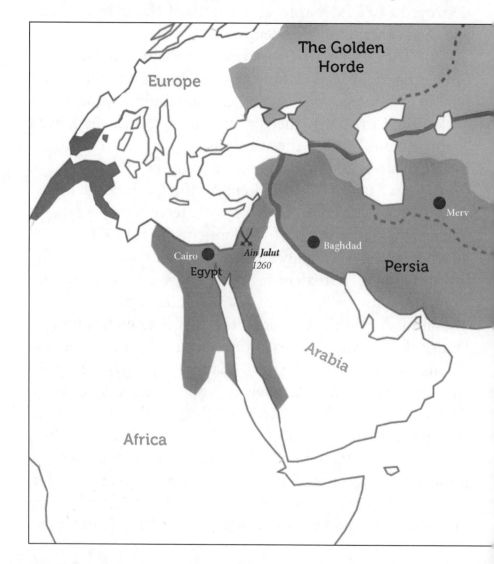

the comparatively small Damascus—were never seriously threatened. The importance of the Crusades weighed far more heavily in the West.

The rather unsophisticated European knights were faced with a life that very much stood out from the cold austerity they faced at home. A certain courtly and economic refinement flowed from the East to the West as a result of the two centuries of contact. Europe benefited to some extent from the Crusades even though its adventure ended in defeat.

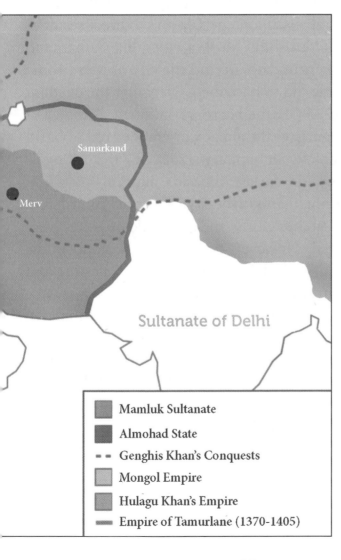

Samarkand

Merv

Sultanate of Delhi

■ Mamluk Sultanate
■ Almohad State
- - Genghis Khan's Conquests
□ Mongol Empire
■ Hulagu Khan's Empire
▬▬ Empire of Tamurlane (1370-1405)

The Mongol Storm (1240–1261)

More spectacular than the Crusades was the chaos inflicted almost at the same time by the Mongol onslaught against the Muslim world. Since the twelfth century CE this nomadic people had erupted with impetuous from the plains of Central Asia simultaneously to the east, south, and west. In 1215 CE Beijing was captured; in 1220 CE, the Muslim state ruled by the Khwarazmian Dynasty was crushed by the Mongols under their leader Genghis Khan; his grandson, Batu, subjugated the Russian principalities in 1237 to 1240 CE; a German-Polish army was defeated in 1241 CE at Legnitz in modern-day Poland. Nevertheless, the Mongols focused their wrath on the Middle East, and in time, even came to adopt the religion of their conquered subjects.

The ravages of the Mongols were unprecedented. Millions of Muslims in Central Asia alone perished as a direct result of their depredations. Flourishing Muslim cities, like Samarkand and Herat, sank into ruin, and around the city of Merv some 1.3 million people are said to have died. Even after the death of Genghis Khan in 1227 CE, the horrors continued. Another of his grandsons, Hulagu, gave the already disempowered Abbasid Caliphate its deathblow. In January 1258 CE, the Mongols conquered the capital and the last Abbasid Caliph, al-Mu'tasim, and at least 800,000 inhabitants of the city were cruelly murdered. Incalculable artistic, architectural, and academic treasures were maliciously destroyed. However, the Mamlukes stopped the invaders in 1260 CE at Ain Jalut in the north of Palestine and prevented them from crossing into Egypt.

Hulagu created a grand Mongol Khanate out of the area of present-day Iraq and Iran. His successors, the Ilkhans, eventually embraced Islam and from their capital of Tabriz even sponsored a revival of Persian culture. In the early fourteenth century, however, the Ilkhan Dynasty collapsed under the pressure of Turks, Byzantines, and Afghans.

Al-Andalus: Eight Centuries of Muslim Spain (711–1492 CE):

As the Abbasid Caliphate sank ingloriously into turmoil, there flourished in the far west of the former empire a lonely dominion of Muslims: Al-Andalus, present-day Spain and Portugal. It was not until 1492 (the year Spain discovered the New World), that this most brilliant of eras came to an end.

Whether the Arabs actually intended to invade the Iberian Peninsula at the beginning of the eighth CE century remains unclear. Regardless, a skillful commanding officer named Tariq ibn Ziyad crossed the Strait of Gibraltar (which is named after him) in 712 CE with 7,000 mostly Berber warriors. Prior to the invasion, a certain renegade Christian nobleman, named Julian, encouraged the Muslim governor of Morocco (Musa bin Nusayr) to come and help him in a revolt against the oppressive Visigoth king of Spain.

The invasion came and the king was slain in battle by Tariq's army. Soon after, the important cities of Córdoba and Toledo fell to the Muslims. The following year, a far larger army of 18,000 men conquered Seville and Merida. Only in the far north, in Asturias, did resistance continue. In 719 CE, the Muslims crossed the Pyrenees, and by 725 CE, they had captured the southern French towns of Narbonne, Nîmes, and Carcassonne. A foray into the Frankish Empire failed in 732 CE at the Battle of Tours, and in 751 CE, the Franks succeeded in driving the Muslims back across the Pyrenees.

During this period, the power of the caliphate was in the hands of the Abbasids. Abd ur-Rahman, the only survivor of the massacre of the Umayyads, fled to the Iberian Peninsula. The son of a Berber woman, he received support from North African Berber troops and, in 756 CE, he was able to prevail against the Abbasid governor.

Abd al-Rahman I established his capital at Córdoba, and he took the title of amir, rather than caliph. Under Abd ur-Rahman III (d. 961 CE), the Muslims were again making forays north of the Pyrenees, even reaching the area around what is now Geneva. Abd al-Rahman III decided to drop the title of amir and resume the loftier title of Caliph of Córdoba. Now there were two rival caliphates in the Muslim world.

Meanwhile, the Christian counterattack—the legendary Reconquista—was brewing in the northern areas of what is now Spain. The kingdoms of Leon and Asturias destroyed a Muslim army near Madrid in 939 CE, and by the mid-tenth century, Muslim military and political influence in Western Europe began to slowly decline.

Although the political and military influence was diminishing, Muslim cultural influence stayed intact, for science and art flourished throughout al-Andalus. The library of Córdoba alone is said to have held some half a million manuscripts. Men of learning from all over Western Europe traveled to Muslim Spain in order to partake in the vast learning stored there. These men returned home with new thoughts, which in turn slowly advanced Western Christian society.

During the zenith of Muslim Iberia, origin and religion mattered little when it came to societal interactions or personal advancement. Christians, Muslims, and Jews worked together in each other's realms and, as elsewhere, Christian and Muslim worlds were by no means in a state of constant war. Rather, there was often a lively exchange of goods and ideas fostered by the religious tolerance and mutual acceptance.

As the power of the caliph fell, a vizier named Almansor (al-Mansur billah) became the de facto ruler of Muslim Iberia. Almansor launched a series of military campaigns against the Christian north. Even though these were successful, they brought about serious consequences, namely the aligning of the previously divided Christian kingdoms in an objective to eradicate Islam from the Iberian Peninsula.

After the death of Almansor in 1002 CE, the Caliphate of Córdoba began to crumble. Tensions between the various Muslim ethnic groups (Arabs, Berbers, and Iberians) led to bloodshed and by the middle of the eleventh century, Muslim Spain had fragmented into a number of small bickering states.

The Christian north, of course, took advantage of this opportunity. Pope Alexander II sanctioned a Crusade against the "Moors" (as Iberian Muslims were known) and a united Castile and Aragón marched against the splintered Muslim lands. In 1085 CE, King Alfonso VI conquered the important city of Toledo, an act that caused the Iberian Muslims to call on the Almoravids (al-Murabitun), a puritanical Moroccan state, to cross the straits and come to their aid. In 1086 CE, the Almoravids achieved a decisive victory over the Christians at the Battle of Sagrajas. This dynasty ruled over Muslim Iberia for some sixty years until they were displaced by another fundamentalist movement from North Africa: the Almohads (al-Muwahhidun). However, the rigid faith of the Almohads could not prevent the loss of Lisbon in 1184 CE and the crushing defeat inflicted upon them by the Christians at the Battle of Las Navas de Tolosa in 1212 CE.

All of Muslim Portugal and Spain was lost at this point, except for a small area around Granada, which continued under the rule of the Nasirid Dynasty. The endurance of the last Muslim bastion lasted until the dynastic union of Castile and Aragón in 1479 CE. In 1491 CE, some 80,000 Christian soldiers laid siege to Granada, which fell the following year. The last Muslim king of Spain, Abu Abdallah (Boabdil), went into exile in Morocco.

With the entire Iberian Peninsula in Christian hands, the Inquisition had free rein to cleanse it of all heresy and unbelief. The Church first drove out the approximately 170,000 Jews, many of whom migrated to Muslim lands. In 1525, all remaining Muslims were given the choice to convert or leave. Those thousands who decided to remain and convert became known as Moriscos, or "Little Moors." All Moriscos (about half a million) were forced in 1614 CE out of the country on the grounds that they were unreliable Christians who had sympathized with the Arabs and Turks. Most settled in Morocco and Tunisia.

The Reconquista was now followed by conquests further abroad. Spain and Portugal succeeded in establishing numerous bases on the North African coast. However, these were completely lost for the most part when the Ottomans reached the region. Henceforth, Spain turned its attention to the conquest of the New World, which Columbus had discovered for the Spanish crown in 1492 CE.

Rise, Fall, and National Rebirth of the Turks

The Turks were a nomadic people of Central Asia. They came into contact with Islam early on, as Arab armies penetrated into what is now eastern Iran and Uzbekistan. Until that time, most Turkish tribes were nominally under Chinese domination. In the following years, more and more Turkish tribes moved westward and as they did so, most of them adopted Islam as their faith. Like the Persians, the Turks retained their language and many cultural peculiarities.

As we mentioned above, during the tenth century a Turkish tribe known as the Seljuks entered the grand stage of Islamic history. Their chief, Tugrul Beg, took Baghdad in 1055 CE and abolished the rule of the Persian Shiite Buyid Dynasty and forced the Abbasid Caliph to make him sultan, thereby appointing him as the secular ruler of the Muslims.

In the decades that followed, the Seljuks subjugated the entire Middle East, but most areas were soon lost again, crumbling into loose tribal confederations. However, Seljuk rule remained strong in central Anatolia (modern Turkey), where the sultans established their capital in the city of Konya. The Byzantines and Crusaders tried in vain to expel the invaders from their former heartland, but the Turks stood firm. The sultanate finally broke under the pressure of the Ilkhans of Persia and other local potentates trying to form their own states.

The Mamluk Sultanate (1250–1517 CE)

Mamluk literally means "property"—an Arabic designation for a male slave. The term is most commonly used to refer to Muslim slave-soldiers and Muslim rulers of slave origin. The Mamluks arose in Egypt during the military crisis provoked by the Seventh Crusade [see page 81] and the Mongol invasion of Syria [see page 85], replacing their former masters, the Ayyubids, and ruled for two and a half centuries.

The Mamluks originated from a Turkish military household of the Ayyubid ruler al-Malik al-Salih Najam in Egypt and Damascus. They were mainly Turks from the southern Russian steppes (Bahriyya who ruled from 1250–1390 CE) and Chechens from the northern Caucasus (Burjis who ruled from 1382–1517 CE). Mamluks embraced and promoted Sunni Islam and defended its holy places such as the Dome of the Rock in Jerusalem and the two great mosques in Makkah and Madinah.

Mamluks became involved in a war with the Ottoman Turks, who captured Cairo in 1517. The Mamluks favored the cavalry and personal combat with sword and shield. They were no match for the Ottomans, who skillfully used artillery. The Ottoman ruler, Selim I, put an end to the Mamluk sultanate and established a small Ottoman garrison in Egypt.

Ottoman Expansion (1501–1924 CE)

The reign of the Turkish clan chief, Osman I (1288–1326), marks the beginning of the great Ottoman Empire. Osman's tribe had originally settled in northwestern Anatolia, along the frontier between Islam and the Byzantine Empire. Given that the Byzantine Empire was at that time in a defensive struggle in the Balkans with the Bulgarians and Serbs, the Turks saw an opportunity to expand into southeastern Europe. In 1349 CE, Orhan, son of Osman I, married the daughter of the Byzantine emperor, who hoped to form a partnership with the tribe.

The next ruler, Murad, gained enough strength to make what remained of the Byzantine Empire a vassal. He defeated the Bulgarian king and inflicted a decisive defeat on the Serbs

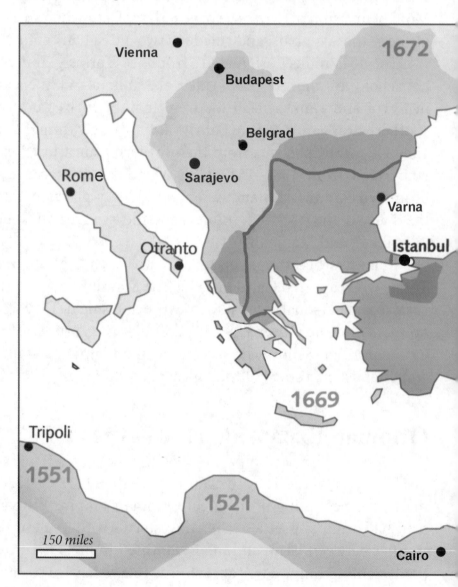

at the Battle of Kosovo in 1389 CE. Although Murad fell in battle, the victory paved the way for Ottoman domination of the Balkans and Hungary. Murad's son, Beyazid I, subjugated the whole of Bulgaria and Greece. A Hungarian army of

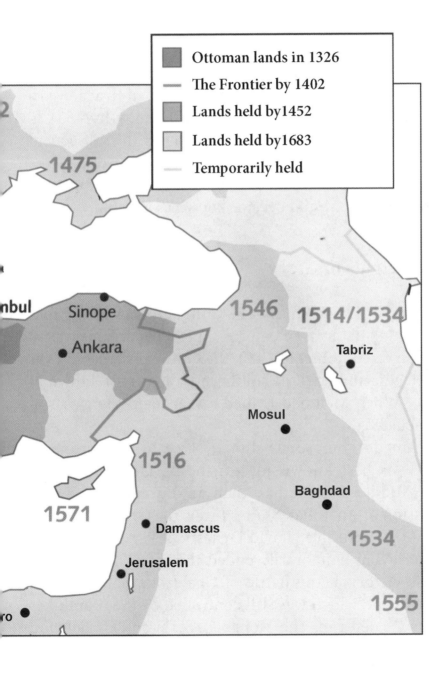

Crusaders tried to stem the tide but they were beaten at the Battle of Nicopolis in 1396 CE.

In 1402, the second Mongol invasion of Tamerlane defeated Beyazid at the Battle of Ankara. Beyazid I died in captivity and Tamerlane restored the small Turkish principalities in Anatolia at the expense of the Ottomans. Civil war followed not long after until Sultan Murad II made successful moves to recapture many lost territories. A Crusader army was defeated at Varna in 1444 CE, and Murad's son, Mehmed II, achieved a long sought after victory over Eastern Christianity. In 1453 CE, the Ottomans stormed Constantinople. Over the subsequent decades and centuries, this city was to become one of the greatest urban centers in all of Islam. It became the capital of the Ottoman Empire and became known as Istanbul.

To the Heights of Glory

Mehmed II (known as "The Conqueror") was the first ruler to think in terms of empire. One of his dreams was to even push on to Rome. In 1480, the Ottomans crossed over from Albania and held the southern Italian coastal town of Otranto. When Mehmed II died a year later, the garrison was evacuated.

Mehmed's grandson, Selim I, came to the throne in 1512. He is best known for expanding Ottoman power in the Middle East rather than in Europe. His harsh suppression of Anatolian Shiites threw the Ottomans into a long conflict with the Safavid Dynasty of Persia, who were Shiites. Having temporarily ended the threat from Persia after his victory at the Battle of Chaldiran, Selim's target became Egypt, which was still controlled by the Mamlukes (famous for defeating the Mongols). Syria quickly fell, and in January 1517 Cairo capitulated due to superior artillery and infantry. Along with Egypt, the Ottomans were also now in control of the holy sites of Mecca and Madinah. The last Abbasid figurehead caliph transferred the title to his much more powerful successors.

The Ottomans penetrated further into North Africa and occupied Algiers in 1518. With the help of local Arabs and Berbers, they destroyed the numerous forts that the Spaniards had established along the coast.

Selim's son, Suleiman I, turned the attention of the empire back to Europe. The chronic hostilities with Hungary were ended at the Battle of Mohacs in 1526 where the Hungarian army was routed and its king slain. In 1529 Sultan Suleiman I carried out the first Ottoman siege of Vienna. The city itself defied the assault and the Ottomans retreated back to the Balkans. Hungary essentially became a no-man's land between the powerful Muslim empire and the Hapsburgs, until 1541 when the Ottomans occupied Budapest. This put Hungary firmly under their control for the next 150 years.

In the east, however, the Ottomans gained other successes by capturing Tabriz and the famed city of Baghdad from the Safavids. In the following years Azerbaijan and other regions of the Caucasus came under direct Ottoman control or influence.

Under Suleiman I, called "the Magnificent" in the West, the Ottoman Empire reached the pinnacle of glory. It spanned not only a huge part of the old Arab caliphate, but also reached far into Christian Europe. Grand constructions—like mosques, palaces, and fortifications—were carried out and the transportation network of the empire was improved. Trade flourished with the general peace that a near-unified Middle East and Balkans afforded

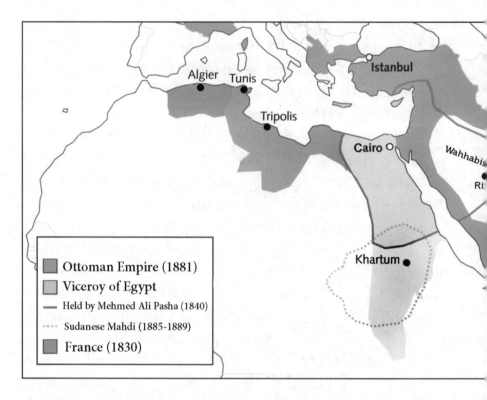

Ottoman Empire (1881)
Viceroy of Egypt
— Held by Mehmed Ali Pasha (1840)
···· Sudanese Mahdi (1885-1889)
France (1830)

people. The powerful empire gave its citizens security and confidence.

Yet, at the same time, the people of Western Europe were entering a new era. The rethinking of Christianity brought about by the Protestant Reformation and the humanistic Renaissance led to a gradual lessening of the grip religion had on not only daily life, but also academic life. In addition, the discovery of new sea routes that led directly to the ports of the Far East eliminated the need for Muslim middlemen and, slowly but surely, the economies of the Middle East began to stagnate and decline.

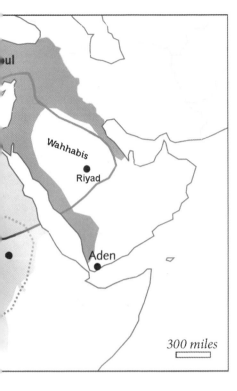

Crisis and Decline

While Holland, England, and France welcomed a capitalist future, the Muslims, for the most part, were stuck in the medieval guild craft tradition. In 1570, Pope Pius V arranged an alliance of Catholic states, known as the Holy League, against the Ottomans. A year later, a combined Spanish and Venetian fleet thoroughly defeated the Turkish navy at Lepanto. This sea battle marked a turning point in Ottoman history. However, disputes among the European powers allowed the empire to survive for another three and a half centuries.

Simultaneously, rebellions shook Anatolia and the Arab territories, and the territorial gains made against Persia were lost in 1619. In Europe, the Ottomans came up against a new and recurring opponent, Russia, which began to expand its sphere of influence in the direction of Ukraine and the Black Sea. Russia would prove to be a thorn in the side of the Ottomans until World War I.

In 1683, a large Turkish army made a second attempt at taking Vienna, only to be driven back by a relief army under the Polish king. From this point onwards, the Ottoman Empire would be on the defensive militarily. In 1686, Budapest fell into the hands of the Hapsburgs, and in 1697 Athens fell to the Venetians. Unable to find any means to check these advances, the Ottomans were made to agree to the Treaty of Karlowitz in 1699. This forced them to surrender most of their lands north of the Danube. The Muslim populations living there were subjected to massacre, forced conversion, or expulsion.

The decline of Ottoman magnificence also had an impact on North Africa. The three statelets of Algeria, Tunisia, and Tripoli intensified their "pirate war" with the Christian states on the opposite side of the Mediterranean. Raid and counter-raid meant that a large number of prisoners from both sides were forced into brutal slavery.

In the eighteenth century Russia became increasingly aggressive. Azov and Kerch were lost, and the Black Sea was no more a "Turkish lake." In addition, the Russians also proclaimed themselves to be the guardians of Orthodox Christianity and protector of those who adhered to the faith. The large Orthodox component of the Ottoman Empire's population instigated episodic rebellions and communal violence. The stability and security of the state was slowly undermined as the Muslim population saw itself surrounded by an increasing number of enemies.

In 1789, a revolution broke out in France that would, over the coming century, affect the entire globe. In that year, Sultan Selim III took the throne. He was the first in a line of Ottoman rulers who wanted to modernize the empire along the European model. Unlike most European countries, there was a lack of a homogeneous society, ethnically and religiously. There were two large religions, Islam and Christianity, both of which contained a myriad of denominations and sects. In addition to religious groups, the Ottoman Empire was home to many ethnicities: Turks, Arabs, Bosnians, Albanians, Circassians (all Muslim) and Greeks, Armenians, Serbs and Bulgarians (all Christians). These differences would become more acute as Western ideas of nationalism began to replace religious solidarity.

In 1798, an army under Napoleon invaded Ottoman Egypt and easily defeated a Muslim army (ill-prepared for modern warfare) in the shadow of the pyramids. Napoleon then headed up the coast of Palestine towards the city of Acre, the last stronghold of the Crusaders five hundred years before. The Ottoman fortress held, however, and the Corsican returned to France in 1799 to seize power. In the wake of the French invasion, Muhammad Ali, an Ottoman officer of Albanian ethnicity, removed the local feudal lords and made himself ruler of Egypt (although for a while in the name of the sultan). At the behest of the Ottoman government, Muhammad Ali successfully checked the advance of the puritanical Wahhabi/Salafi sect that had emerged out of the interior of what is now Saudi Arabia.

One noteworthy event during the first half of the nineteenth century was the proclamation of the "Supreme Edict of the Rose Palace" (Hatti Serif) in 1839. This decree guaranteed all subjects, no matter their religion or ethnicity, the inviolability of person and property. This was part of the Tanzimât (reorganization) reforms, designed to bring the Ottoman state in line with the increasingly secularized West.

In addition to the complete Westernization of the military in 1826, steps were taken to modernize the educational system and, in 1845, the first modern Turkish university was opened (although it would not be until 1870 that one was opened in Istanbul). The longed-for liberation of the peasant class from the old feudal system was still slow in coming, even though it was called for by the reforms. The displacement of Muslim privilege encouraged the non-Muslim bourgeoisie to begin organizing movements for the establishment of their own independent nation states, at the expense of the Ottoman Empire. Greece declared its independence in 1821 and Serbia in 1833, both states expelling or eradicating its Muslim population.

Yet, the empire remained economically weak and hence inferior militarily and politically. Russia exploited this weakness and attacked the Ottoman Empire in 1853, sparking what would be called the Crimean War. Even though the empire was saved from total destruction by the intervention of its allies Britain and France, it still lost parts of eastern Anatolia to its powerful northern neighbor.

Despite all the advances in modernization, the state remained absolutist at its core and a growing number of Western-educated Muslim intellectuals felt that reforms had not gone far enough. They founded the movement known as the "Young Ottomans," and in 1876, they forced the sultan to sign a constitution that they had composed. This was the first modern constitution put into effect outside of the Western world.

However, the constitution was suspended in the wake of the Russian invasion of 1877. After nearly two years of fighting, the Ottomans would have been on the verge of a complete collapse had the Western powers not intervened. Millions of Muslims were displaced in the Balkans and the Caucasus region, and hundreds of thousands were killed. The Treaty of San Stefano and the Congress of Berlin saved the empire, but the Ottomans lost almost the entire Balkans except Albania, Macedonia, and Trace. The French annexed Tunisia in 1881 and in 1882 Egypt came under the "protection" of Britain.

The Ottomans in the World War I

Between 1911 and 1913, Libya (the last African possession of the Ottomans) was lost to Italy, and an alliance of Balkan states drove out the Turks from nearly all of Europe. During World War I (1914–1918), the Ottomans allied themselves with Germany and Austria-Hungary, particularly to counter the growing expansion of Russia. In August 1914, Istanbul and Berlin signed a secret military agreement. In the general mobilization, the Ottoman government called four million men to take up arms; but in reality such a number was unrealistic given the exhaustion of the Muslim public from the very recent wars with Italy and the Balkan states.

During the war, internal strains boiled over. Hoping for a separate nation, the religious leader of the Armenians, the Catholicos, called on his ethnic kinsmen to rise up against the Ottomans and collaborate with the invading Russian army. In the wake of the advance of the Czar's forces into Anatolia, ghastly massacres of tens of thousands of Muslims were carried out by the Christian Armenian population as they planned for their ethnically pure state. Fearing the horrendous bloodshed that would follow, the Ottoman government decided to deport en masse all Armenians living along the front lines in eastern Anatolia. With the dire wartime situation and lack of resources, it is estimated that between 1915 and 1916 some one million Armenians died from starvation, exhaustion, and massacre when they were forced into exile to other parts of the empire.

While the Turks tried in vain to hold back the Russian juggernaut in Anatolia and successfully blocked an Allied landing at Gallipoli, rebellion broke out among their fellow Muslims in Arabia. In 1916, the Ottoman governor of Mecca (the Sharif) succumbed to intrigue and allied with the British. The British promised Arab leaders an independent and united Arabia freed from the Ottomans. However, the Arabs did not know that such promises were useless, as the British and French had already secretly agreed to divide up the Arab world between them.

Sykes-Picot and the Illusion of Arab Freedom

In May 1916, the British government (represented by Sir Mark Sykes) concluded with France (represented by Francois G. Picot) an agreement that marked out the spheres of influence of both countries in an anticipated post-Ottoman Middle East. London and Paris planned to divide the region between their respective nations. At the same time, the British encouraged the tribes of the Arabian Peninsula to act in their own interests, against the Turks.

To organize the Arab resistance, a British officer named T.E. Lawrence ("Lawrence of Arabia") traveled to the Hejaz. Jeddah and Mecca were seized from the Turks, the important Hejaz railway was suspended and, finally, the port of Aqaba was conquered. However, the revolt was regionally restricted to the northwest of Arabia. The British played a game during this time of not only double-crossing the Arab resistance, but also triple-crossing them. The British desired to secure parts of northern Arabia as a colony, guaranteeing Arab leaders independence, all the while promising Jewish Zionists a homeland in Palestine.

In 1917, Foreign Minister Balfour agreed that his government would allow for a Jewish homeland in the Middle East after the war. In 1919 the son of the Sharif's son, Faisal, met with the Zionist leader, Chaim Weizmann in Syria. Both parties agreed, in principle, to accept the Balfour Declaration. However, failure to fully carry out the points of the agreement sparked later conflict between Jews and Arabs, conflict which continues to this day.

At the end of World War I in 1918, the Ottoman Empire was not only deprived of all of its Arab territories, but the victors occupied large tracts of Anatolia, seen as the Turkish heartland. It was only through the resolute Mustafa Kemal

Pasha that the state did not completely collapse. He managed to reorganize the remnants of the Ottoman army in order to liberate all of Anatolia from the invaders.

In 1919, neighboring Greece invaded western Anatolia with the dream of establishing a "Greater Greece." Tens of thousands of Muslims were once again massacred and tens of thousands more made refugees. After a long and bitter war, the Turkish army, under Mustafa Kemal's command, drove the Greeks back to the Aegean Sea. When the tide turned against the Greeks during the course of the war, a mass exodus of Greeks from Anatolia began. The Treaty of Lausanne ended the conflict and it also called for a population exchange between Turkey and Greece. About 500,000 Muslims (mostly ethnic Turks, Greeks, and Albanians) were expelled from Greece and resettled in Anatolia, while roughly a million Anatolian Greeks were moved to Greece.

The Ottoman sultanate was abolished at the end of 1922 and the Turkish Republic came into being a year later. In 1924, a further blow to tradition came with the abolition of the office of the caliphate.

The Kemalist Republic

Having established his power as the first leader of the Republic of Turkey, Mustafa Kemal changed his name to Atatürk, "Father of the Turks." Atatürk pushed his compatriots to keep pace with the twentieth-century West. The new republic was secularized with a strict separation of Islam and state. The many Sufi orders were outlawed and a number of sweeping (and often radical) social changes were set in place: the official use of the Gregorian calendar, the Latin alphabet replaced the Arabic script for writing Turkish, and the face veil (but not the scarf, or hijab), polygamy, and even the fez were banned. Ottoman law, which was heavily based on the Shari'ah, was replaced with the Swiss civil code.

At the same time, in an effort to create a national identity and weaken historic ties to the broader Muslim world, the Turkish nation and its language was glorified beyond all measure. Yet, all of these modernization efforts could not alter Turkey's Islamic character.

Despite a clear connection with the modern world and the West (Turkey became a member of NATO in 1952), narrow-mindedness in regards to Turkey and the Turks continues to run high in Europe.

The Turkic Dynasties of Persia

Like the rulers of ancient times, the Safavid leaders (though Turkic) were given the title of Shah. Unlike the Ottomans, the Safavids were ardent Shiites, and they imposed this brand of Islam—by force or otherwise—on the predominantly Sunni population of Persia. After the Ottomans defeated them at the Battle of Chaldiran in 1514, which resulted in the fall of Tabriz, the Safavids chose the city of Isfahan as the new seat of government. With this shift in capitals, the Safavids became more Persianized, and by the time of Shah Abbas I (1587–1629), the ethnic Persian domination was secured at the expense of their fellow Turkic tribesmen. Due to the incessant hostilities with the Sunni Ottomans, the once lucrative transit trade between Europe, India, and China via Persia virtually came to a standstill. Economic decline and social stagnation quickly followed. Not even reclaiming the important port of Hormuz from the Portuguese in 1622 changed this grave situation.

The Safavid Empire fell in 1722 to the gradually encroaching Afghans, and then after that to another Turkic dynasty, the Afsharids, whose leader Nadir Shah was able to temporarily extend his sphere of influence to Delhi and Bukhara. Nadir Shah made a remarkable move of trying to reconcile Sunnis and Shiites within his realm, although this was met with little enthusiasm from the clergy of both sects.

After barely sixty years in power, the Afsharid Dynasty was bankrupted by the continual wars with their eastern neighbors. In 1796, yet another tribe of Turkic origin—the Qajars—came to the throne and made Tehran the new capital of Persia. The country could barely maintain even nominal independence as the expanding European powers exerted influence in the region. From the north the Russian Empire repeatedly tried to gain power and after 1813, its frontiers reached the northwestern borders of Persia. Britain came to exert its influence in the Persian Gulf and it especially succeeded in the Persian economic sector, and over the course of the nineteenth century, these two powers would come to dictate the destiny of Persia.

Early Muslim influence in India

By the eighth century, Arab armies had reached the Indus River. At first they penetrated eastward only to make raids and there were no serious attempts to settle in the northern plains of the subcontinent. The Ghaznavid Empire (which was centered in Afghanistan) began pushing into northwest India and by 1025 CE most of the Punjab had come under their control. Some two centuries later, Afghan slave-soldiers founded the

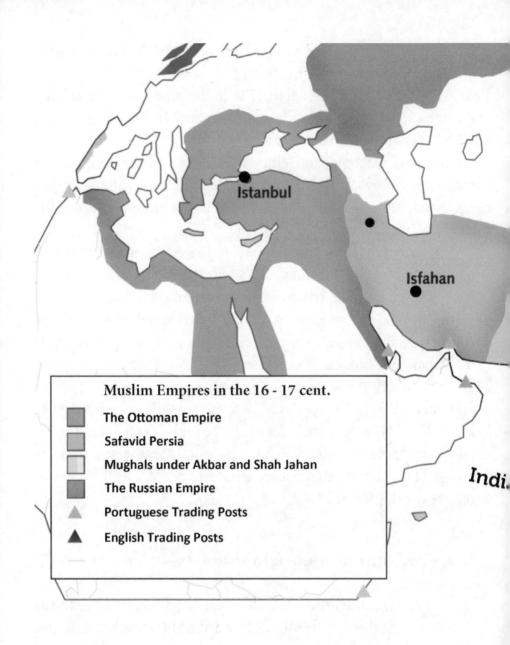

Muslim Empires in the 16 - 17 cent.

- The Ottoman Empire
- Safavid Persia
- Mughals under Akbar and Shah Jahan
- The Russian Empire
- Portuguese Trading Posts
- English Trading Posts

Sultanate of Delhi. Over the next three centuries, this state ebbed and flowed over much of the Indian subcontinent, allowing for a rich mingling of Hindu and Muslim cultures. The

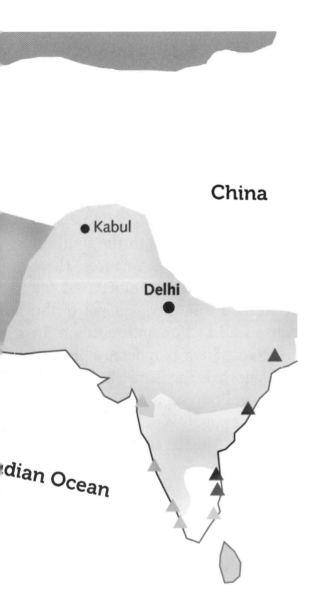

Sultanate of Delhi fell into decline after its army was crushed in 1398 by the invading Tamerlane. However, the rule of the famed conqueror over India was short and his successor could not keep the country from fragmenting into minor Sunni, Shiite, and Hindu states.

The Mughal Empire (1526–1857 CE)

The founder of this remarkable Muslim dynasty that ruled over India was Babur, a descendant of both Tamerlane and Genghis Khan. Originally the lord of the fertile Fergana Valley in Central Asia, his power expanded far to the south, and he took Delhi and Agra in 1526. His grandson, the famed Akbar, who ruled between 1556 and 1605, followed a curious zigzag policy in matters of faith, hovering between subjugation and tolerance of other religions. Nevertheless, he greatly expanded Mughal rule.

Shah Jahan (1627–1658) became perhaps the most famous ruler of the dynasty. Militarily, he was rather unsuccessful, as he failed in an attempt to conquer the Central Asian homeland of his ancestors. However, he triggered a building boom; the famous Red Fort of Delhi and the Taj Mahal—the tomb of his wife and one of the most beautiful buildings not only of Islam but also of the entire world—were among his achievements.

The luxurious palaces and endless wars in the south of the subcontinent, however, ruined the public finances. These economic problems and the increasing resentment of the Hindu masses at being ruled by a minority segment of the population led to persistent dissatisfaction and rebellion. In 1739, the above-mentioned Nadir Shah plundered northern India, and Afghan invasions followed. The British and French increasingly sought to exploit the ailing empire to their benefit. The last Mughal rulers were only puppets kept in power by the benevolence of the British. The last Mughal emperor, Bahadur Shah Zafar, died in exile in 1862.

The Era of European Colonialism (1800–1950 CE)

The breakdown of the Ottoman Empire was accompanied by the advance of European armies into Muslim lands: first, North Africa, then the peripheries of the Arabian Peninsula, and eventually to South and Southeast Asia. Many experts like to point to the Crusades as the root of modern-day Muslim indignity; yet this event is too far back in time. The root of this humiliation should rather be sought in the modern age—with the coming of colonialism and neocolonialism.

The French in North Africa

The first victim of the European colonization was Algeria in North Africa. French troops invaded Algeria in 1830 and by 1843 it was declared French-owned. Paris brought radical changes to their new colony without regard for the traditional structures that had existed there for centuries. The best agricultural land went to French settlers, who numbered more than 350,000 people in 1901. These Christians (and some 50,000 Jews) enjoyed full rights as French citizens. The approximately four million Arabs and Berbers were second-class citizens.

Resistance circled around the Arab chieftain Amir Abdul Qadir (1807–1883). In 1835 and 1836, he defeated several French units and freed portions of Algeria. A French counterattack in 1842 forced Abdul Qadir to flee into Morocco and in 1844 his reorganized army suffered a heavy defeat. In 1847, he was captured by the French and exiled to the Levant, far from home, where he died in 1883.

From Algeria, the French moved onwards to capture Tunisia (1881) and much of Morocco. Libya was seized from the Ottoman Empire in 1911, although the local population resisted for quite some time.

Great Britain in Egypt and Arabia

More subtle methods of control appealed to the British. Though they occupied Egypt in 1882, they left the country's status as a tributary state of the Ottoman Empire, under the nominal reign of the Khedive (or viceroy), untouched. This state of affairs lasted until the beginning of World War I in 1914.

Egypt was strategically important for London, since control of the Suez Canal (which opened in 1869) was vital. This busy waterway generated enormous economic might, though only a fraction of Egyptians benefited from it.

The British also secured spheres of influence on the periphery of the Arabian Peninsula. In 1839, they occupied Aden and the Yemeni hinterland, and by 1891, they had treaties with local potentates in Oman and Bahrain. In 1899, the global empire absorbed the emirate of Kuwait. Yet, the interior of the peninsula remained under the control of Arab tribes, primarily that of the Saudis.

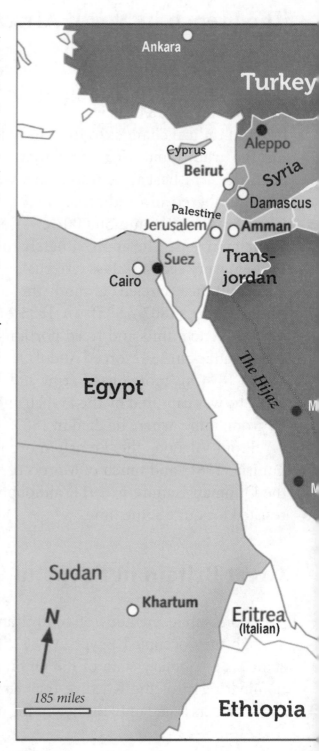

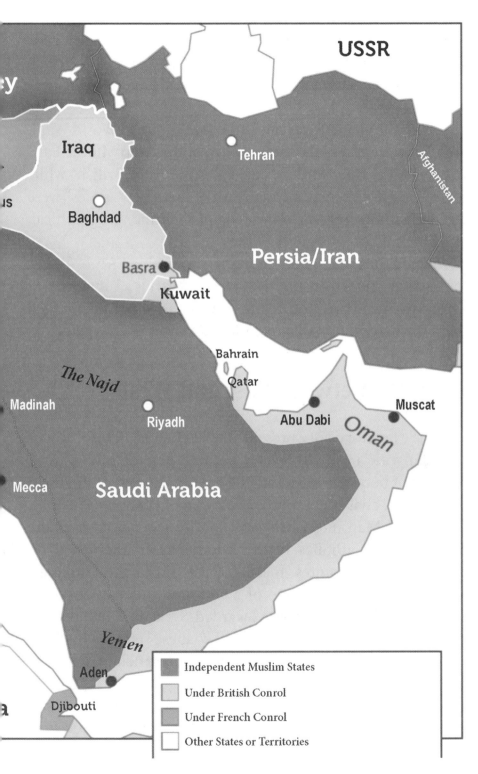

After the occupation of the whole of India in 1858, the Muslims of the subcontinent came under European rule. Through protracted and extremely costly wars, the British succeeded in occupying adjoining Afghanistan between 1833 and 1842.

With the victory over the Ottoman Empire in World War I, both Britain and France took control of the Arab Middle East. In the 1920s, Iraq, Jordan, and Palestine were British, while Syria became a French mandate. All of these new "states" were created without regard to the religious, ethnic, geographical, or historical circumstances of the

region, leaving them extremely unstable. Accordingly, the French created in tiny Lebanon an artificial majority of Christians in opposition to the Muslims, which guaranteed them the longest possible retention of power in the region.

Lebanon Between East and West

The territory of present-day Lebanon came under Ottoman rule in 1516; it later became part of Muhammad Ali's Egypt between 1831 and 1840. After the end of Egyptian occupation, civil war broke out between Lebanon's Muslims, Druze, and Maronite Christians. France (seeing itself as the champion of Catholics in the Middle East) intervened on behalf of the Maronites. In 1860 Paris forced the Ottomans to allow Lebanon a degree of autonomy under a Christian governor. When France was awarded Syria as a mandate in 1920, it drew the borders of a new Lebanese state, giving it a

narrow Maronite majority. Thus an artificial Christian-dominated state was created in the Middle East. At the beginning of World War II, Allied units occupied Syria and Lebanon, and in September 1941, both countries received independence. Nevertheless, the French tried again in May 1945 to recover control by force of arms, but the UN stopped this attempt. The proportional representation between Christians (of various sects) and Muslims (of various sects) broke up over time, and the tensions between the religious groups eventually escalated into bloody civil war.

World War II and the Collapse of Colonial Empires (1950 CE–Today)

When World War II broke out in 1939, the Arab and wider Muslim world felt its effects. In 1941, Italian and German troops tried to push through Egypt to the Suez Canal from Libya. The Battle of El Alamein in November 1942 was the turning point in the war, and the Axis forces were compelled to retreat through Libya and then Tunisia. Many civilians in these lands lost their lives during the combat.

Encouraged by the initial successes of the Axis powers, a rebellion broke out against the British in Iraq in May 1941; however, this was quickly brought under control. That same year, British and Soviet troops occupied Iran, because its ruler, Reza Shah, was becoming increasingly pro-German.

Although the British and French were on the winning side at the end of the war in 1945, both were heavily damaged. In particular, the British economy had suffered from hard years of war, and a severe economic crisis shook the empire. This is the prime reason for Britain's decision to withdraw from many of its territorial holdings around the world. Yet, this was done rather haphazardly and often with disastrous consequences for the respective regions.

The Palestinian Question

The first of these withdrawals was the ending of the British Mandate in Palestine. From 1882, Jews—mostly from Eastern Europe—began settling in this Ottoman-ruled land. The World Zionist Organization, a Jewish nationalist movement, encouraged this colonization. The goal was the creation of a "Jewish national home" in Palestine. After all, the land between the Jordan River and the Mediterranean Sea had once been the origin of Judaism two thousand years in the past. Obviously, in the interim, other peoples had settled in Palestine, and by the twentieth century the land had long held an Arab majority.

Undeterred by the historical and demographic realities, the Zionists continued to pursue their goal. After World War I, the British became the new lords over the country, and both Arabs and Jews held hopes for an independent state. Already in 1921 there were clashes between Jews and Arabs. In 1882, only 24,000 Jews lived in Palestine, but by 1930 there were 80,000. Jews purposefully built their own political and economic infrastructure; already 14 percent of cultivable land had been bought, and more and more Arabs were displaced from public office. After Hitler came to power in Germany, Jewish immigration to Palestine increased by leaps and bounds. The Arabs increased their rioting; riots that were quelled by British troops and Jewish militias.

From 1939, the British tried to curb Jewish immigration to Palestine as much as possible. However, in the wake of World War II, pressure increased on the British and Arabs to accept the establishment of a Jewish state.

In January 1947, Churchill declared that Britain desired to resign from the League of Nations mandate of Palestine. The newly established United Nations formed a Palestine

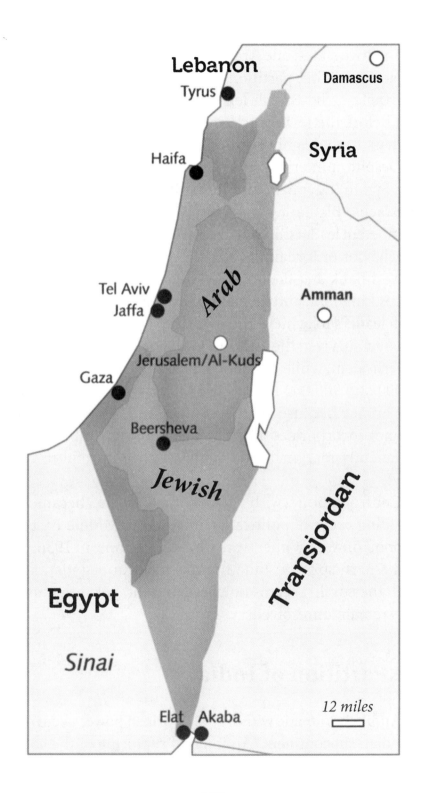

117

Committee (UNSCOP), which oversaw the division of the land into two states: one Arab and one Jewish. While the Jewish side accepted this partition, the Arabs rejected it outright. Nevertheless, the British left Palestine on May 15, 1948, the night before the Jews proclaimed the State of Israel. The new country's Arab neighbors promptly declared war.

Despite numerical superiority, the combined Lebanese, Iraqi, Syrian, Egyptian, and Jordanian armies failed to defeat the Israelis. Blame lay not only with military inexperience, incompetent leadership, and lack of coordination, but also with the behavior of Jordan. Its ruler, King Abdullah, desired that the West Bank and the holy city of Jerusalem be incorporated into his kingdom, and he had no problem in negotiating with Israeli leaders to achieve these goals.

Israel survived the war, and Jordan received the West Bank and Jerusalem, while Egypt occupied the Gaza Strip. Between 700,000 and 900,000 Palestinian Muslims and Christians lost their homes because of the conflict and, as refugees, they were not incorporated into the neighboring Arab states, but permanently marginalized (many still live in refugee camps today).

Confrontation with Israel henceforth became the overriding cause of political conflict in the Middle East from this point onward. Other wars were yet to come: in 1956, 1967, and 1973. In spite of some improvement in negotiations, an end to the conflict seems nowhere in sight, given that its core issues remain unresolved.

The Partition of India

Another dramatic withdrawal of British power occurred on the Indian subcontinent. An internal rupturing of the country

started to take place as early as 1906. In that year, the All India Muslim League split from the Indian National Congress, which had existed since 1885. While the secular-oriented Congress Party (though Hindu-dominated) strove for the independence of a united India, the Muslim League pushed for a separate state for India's Muslim population: Pakistan ("Land of the Pure"). Neither the British nor the charismatic Mahatma Gandhi were able to defuse the conflict between the parties. In August of 1946 some five thousand died in Calcutta from communal rioting between Muslims and Hindus.

Lord Mountbatten—the last British Viceroy of India— finally presented a partition plan that the Congress Party and Muslim League accepted. The division of India triggered a mass exodus and expulsion: Muslims flocked to the newly created Pakistan, and Hindus to India. Approximately twelve million people had to find new homes, while 800,000 to one million Muslims, Hindus, and Sikhs were killed.

An ongoing conflict between the two new states focused on the region of Kashmir. Because Kashmir was populated predominantly by Muslims, it was believed that it should have gone to Pakistan. However, its last Maharaja was Hindu and therefore India laid claim to the region. The demarcation line of 1949 became the northern border of the two countries, but in 1965 conflict flared. With China as a neighbor (which warred with India in 1962), three nuclear powers stand facing each other with very different interests. This makes Kashmir a focal point that is of more than regional importance.

The Algerian War of Independence

In North Africa, the colonial era, likewise, ended in disaster. Here, the Algerians vigorously demanded independence from France. Already in May 1945, there were mass protests by Algerians that were bloodily suppressed by the French colonial authorities. An estimated 10,000 Muslims were killed in the repression. In November 1954, the National Liberation Front (FLN) under Ahmed Ben Bella began to launch attacks against the French. Approximately 30,000 FLN fighters resisted the might of the French army until 1956. The war went on, and great brutality was inflicted on the civilian population, with whole villages razed to the ground. Militarily, the FLN was soon on the defensive, but it was increasingly gaining ground politically against France.

French political opinions could have ended the Algerian crisis in 1958, but nationalist French Algerians (pied-noirs) and a number of French army officers saw their position endangered and they staged a coup. They pushed the popular General Charles de Gaulle to the fore in the hope that he would continue the war until victory was achieved. De Gaulle, however, was anxious to quickly end the conflict. In a referendum held in April 1962, more than 90 percent of French citizens approved Algerian independence, which was granted on July 1, 1962. Nearly a million people—the majority of whom were Algerian Muslims—had lost their lives for it.

Muslims in Russia and the Soviet Union

For nearly three hundred years, the extreme east of Europe was oppressed by Mongols, and then later by Muslim Tatars. Only in the sixteenth century did the Grand Duchy of Moscow succeed in shaking off its "Asiatic yoke." As the nucleus of the future of Russia, Moscow came to subdue huge territories in its south and east. Numerous Muslim peoples came under the influence of this economically weak, but politically influential, Christian power.

As a relic of the devastating Mongol expansion of the thirteenth century, Asian steppe peoples settled along the Volga and Don Rivers and in the Crimean Peninsula, where they eventually converted to Islam. While the Khanate of Crimea became an Ottoman vassal state, the khanates of Kazan, Astrakhan, and Sibir maintained their independence. Although their strength abated, they were still strong enough to be recognized by the neighboring Russian principalities. Only under Ivan IV ("the Terrible") did Russia conquer Kazan and Astrakhan. The gateways to Siberia and the Caucasus

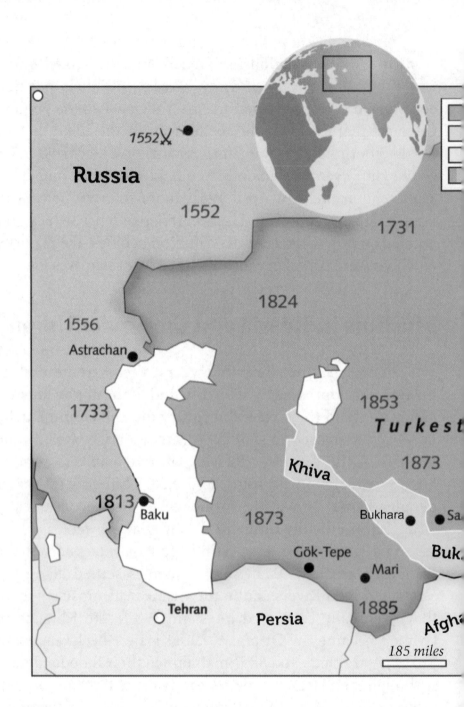

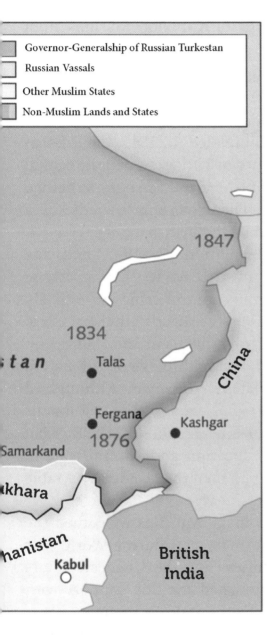

Governor-Generalship of Russian Turkestan

Russian Vassals

Other Muslim States

Non-Muslim Lands and States

were pushed open. However, the Crimean Tatars raided Moscow in 1571, and with Ottoman assistance, they were able to hold out until the eighteenth century.

Until that time, the Russians had already brought forward their borders at the northern edge of the Caucasus and they occupied the northern part of present-day Kazakhstan. The many small and mostly Muslim Caucasian ethnic groups had so far been under Ottoman or Persian influence, and they fought bitterly against the invasion from the north. In their conquests, the Russians gained as allies the Christian Georgians and Armenians.

In the first half of the nineteenth century, an Islamic resistance movement in Daghestan came into being with the aim to push back the Christian advances. The popular Chechen leader, Imam Shamil, succeeded in withstanding the Russians between 1832 and 1859. To secure its southern border the Czar's government took the draconian step of expelling to the Ottoman Empire upwards of a million Muslims from the northern approaches to the Caucasus. Nearly half of this number died on the long march over the mountains or crossing the Black Sea.

At the same time, the Russian conquest of the Muslim states of Central Asia was completed. In 1867, the Russian Empire created a new province of Turkestan with its capital at Tashkent. The khanates of Khiva and Bukhara remained as vassal states to Moscow. The expansion towards India and Persia was only stopped by the British.

After the October Revolution of 1917 and the subsequent establishment of the Soviet Union, those Muslims living under Moscow's control came more firmly under its grip. The new regime was strictly atheistic; Islam suffered as much as Christianity, Judaism, and Buddhism. Mosques were closed, and the faithful were subject to numerous regulations and blatant harassment. Although all nationalities were constitutionally equal, ethnic Russians dominated in the non-Russian Soviet republics. The Russian language was required in education and administration, and the Cyrillic alphabet supplanted the customary Arabic script of Muslim languages.

Due to this oppression, many Muslims welcomed the victorious advance of the German army during World War II. Some Muslim communities, like the Crimean Tatars and the Chechens, were punished for this support with deportation to Central Asia by the Stalinist regime.

The implosion of the Soviet Union in the late 1980s gave the Central Asian states statehood and it prompted the rebirth of Islam in the region. In these countries, however, the governments were filled with former communist party bosses. Fear of destabilizing influences from neighboring Afghanistan and Iran has been used as an excuse by these regimes to repress any opposition. Russia continues to hold enormous political and cultural influence in this region, as it naturally considers its former "backyard" an area of interest. Within its own borders one region has long been an open source of conflict for Russia.

The War in Chechnya

The roots of this ongoing bloody conflict go back centuries, and its causes are complex. With the end of empire, the continued repression of the Chechens by the Russians seemed to end. A so-called Soviet Mountain Republic was established in 1921 that even incorporated elements of the Shari'ah into its legal code. The area around the capital, Grozny, became very important due to rich oil reserves, which covered 17 percent of Russia's demands, even before World War I. Together with the deposits in nearby Azerbaijan, the Soviet Union drew nearly 80 percent of its supply of fossil fuels from this region.

Between 1928 and 1938 Stalinist terror ravaged today's Chechnya. Tens of thousands of wealthy Muslim farmers, clergymen, and members of the intelligentsia fell victim to it. In 1936 the original Mountain Republic had long since been dismantled and shrunk to the Chechen-Ingush Autonomous Soviet Socialist Republic. Resistance to the Soviets grew. In 1942, troops of the German army advanced into the Caucasus, and fighters from the so-called "Special Group of the Caucasian Brothers" began to collaborate with these supposed liberators. At the same time nearly 29,000 Chechens fought on the side of the Red Army against the German invaders.

Nevertheless, Chechens, Ingush, and Daghestanis were considered collaborators by Stalin's regime. In 1944, they were deported en masse to the windswept steppes of Kazakhstan. Of the nearly 460,000 deported, only 200,000 survived long enough to return to their homeland in 1957. As the Soviet Union ended and the new unstable Russia emerged, secessionists in Checheno-Ingushetia saw their opportunity to gain independence. Under the leadership of Dzhokhar Dudayev—a former general in the Soviet strategic bomber fleet—an area roughly the size of Vermont sought to take on the largest military on earth. At the end of 1991, the Chechen Republic was proclaimed, while neighboring Ingushetia remained within the Russian Federation. Russian troops withdrew in 1992, and it was only in 1994 that Moscow decided to intervene. One hundred thousand Russian soldiers blanketed the country with bombs and shelling, achieving little success. The civilian population suffered greatly with as many as 75,000 being killed. Chechen field commanders began to strike behind the lines of Russia's southern flank.

Ultimately, Russian troops occupied Grozny in early 1995. Yet a year later, Chechen guerrillas managed to recapture the city, forcing the Russians to withdraw. By mid-1996, Russian President Yeltsin concluded a hurried peace with the Chechens in order to secure his re-election.

The Chechens failed to build a credible democratic structure in their newly independent state. On the contrary, clan rivalries flourished under the moderate but weak president Aslan Maskhadov. Salafism spread into the land from the Gulf and Afghanistan, and it began to take hold and radicalize elements of the population.

When the Salafist bands tried to invade Russian-controlled Daghistan in 1999, Moscow struck back, this time with overwhelming might. Russian troops attacked Grozny and essentially leveled the city, and large parts of Chechnya were laid waste by the onslaught. All of the gains made in 1996 were undone by the Salafist "mujahidin." Terrorist attacks reached a new high and they focused not only on neighboring republics, but also on the city of Moscow itself. Since 2000, a seemingly endless conflict has been raging on the northern edge of the Caucasus Mountains.

Bosnia and Kosovo

The rugged land of Bosnia and Herzegovina has historically straddled the border between East and West. It marked a boundary between the spheres of influence of the Catholic and the Orthodox Church, and later between Christianity and Islam. In the early fifteenth century, the Ottomans began to send raids into Bosnia, and in 1463 the land came under Muslim rule. Further to the south, Albania also surrendered to the Turks during the same period, however, only after a bitter struggle. Nevertheless, in the coming centuries many among the landed nobility and the common people in these lands—and throughout the Balkans—converted to Islam.

The disintegration of the multi-national state of Yugoslavia in the early years of the 1990s brought calamity to the Muslims in Bosnia (who now represent roughly half of the population). Another latent conflict ignited in the southern Yugoslav region of Kosovo a few years after the war in Bosnia ended.

Bosnia-Herzegovina was a microcosm of Yugoslavia. Here lived Orthodox Serbs, Catholic Croats, and Muslim Bosniaks together in apparent peace. This communist-enforced harmony was broken in 1992 when Bosniaks and Croats voted for independence in a referendum, while the Serbs voted to keep Bosnia in what was left of Yugoslavia. Assisted by Croatia and Serbia, Bosnia's Serb and Croat minorities sought to bring the widest possible area of Bosnia-Hercegovina under their control. The Serbs seized about 70 percent of the country, mostly from fighting, expelling, and slaughtering Muslims. Both Serbs and Croats committed atrocities against the Muslims on a scale that had not been seen in Europe since the end of World War II. In one of the most infamous incidents around the eastern Bosnian town of Srebrenica, Serbs slaughtered upwards of 8,000 Muslim men and boys.

Pressed by the West, the Catholic and Muslim Bosnians allied with each other, but the lopsided alliance broke up in 1993 when the Croats formed their own state called Herceg-Bosna. Henceforth, the Muslims now had to contend with Croats in addition to Serbs. Only renewed international pressure led to a re-established Croat-Muslim coalition, which proved able to stop the Serbian advances.

Since none of the three sides stood any chance of a decisive victory, a peace treaty was signed in 1995 between the warring parties in Dayton, Ohio. According to this agreement, the country would remain intact, but divided into two components: the Muslim-Croat Federation (51 percent of the territory) and the Republika Srpska (48 percent). This arrangement ensured the country's dysfunction without massive international support.

The situation in Kosovo turned out to be another long-simmering inter-ethnic conflict. Serbia viewed Kosovo as a quasi-national shrine. It was here in 1389 that the feudal armies of Serbia were defeated by the Ottomans. For the Serbian nation and the Serbian Orthodox Church, the soil soaked with their blood was henceforth "holy." Demographics, however, were never a point of consideration. On the eve of the collapse of Yugoslavia, the region of Kosovo had 1.8 million inhabitants (1988) of whom some 90 percent were Muslim Albanians. It must be pointed out that when the Ottoman Empire was forced out of this area in 1912 and the borders of new states were drawn, nearly half of all ethnic Albanians

States that once
comprosed the former
Yugoslavia

1 Slovenia
2 Croatia
3 Bosnia-Hercegovina
4 Serbia
5 Montenegro
6 Macedonia

The Federation of
Bosnia-Hercegovina

The Serb Republic

Muslim-majority lands

were left outside of Albania. Much like the arbitrarily drawn borders of the Middle East, this left great room for instability.

The post-communist strongman of Serbia, Slobodan Milosevic, resurrected the myth of Kosovo in order to force the Albanian majority to its knees. As early as 1989, Albanian was no longer an official language, and open discrimination of Muslims became palpable.

The initial non-violent resistance of the Albanian community slowly turned to violence due to their desperation. The massive use of force by the Serbian police and army in the mid-1990s resulted in an intensification of oppression. Finally, in 1999 Belgrade began an all-out assault on several Kosovar towns arresting, expelling, and massacring at will, with the aim of cleansing the entire region of its Muslim population. Tens of thousands of Albanian Muslim civilians fled in abject terror into neighboring Albania and Macedonia. The West was not about to allow a repeat of Bosnia and NATO jets began an intense bombing of Serbian positions.

In June, Belgrade withdrew its troops from Kosovo, and the area came under international administration. The situation has now been reversed. The few remaining Serbs living in Kosovo do so as a powerless minority. In 2008, Kosovo officially declared its independence from Serbia.

Islam in East and Southeast Asia

In Southeast Asia, Islam and Muslim culture was spread mainly by Arab, Persian, and Chinese traders. They found a fertile ground in the Malay Archipelago, where the great Hindu-Buddhist dynasties entered the faith of the Prophet, and with them the masses of their subjects.

By 1300 the first sultanate was established on the island of Sumatra; this state, Aceh, became an early center of Southeast Asian Islam. From the 1400s Islamic principalities formed on the island of Java that grew in both size and power.

The first Europeans reached the Malay Archipelago in the beginning of the sixteenth century, and opened both trade and conflict with the local Muslims. The Dutch prevailed against the Portuguese and the British, and by entering into clever alliances with the rival Muslim states they were able to play one off against the other. By 1596 they had control of the Moluccas and, over the next two centuries, virtually all of the islands of present-day Indonesia. The administration of these holdings was placed in the hands of the Dutch East India Company. After the company's bankruptcy in 1799, control was taken over directly by the Dutch government. Yet, the subjugation of the outer islands proved arduous and bloody. Only after thirty years of war did Aceh yield to the Dutch in 1903, and Hindu-dominated Bali was not incorporated until 1908.

The resistance to the colonial administration began in 1912 with the formation of the Sarekat Islam movement. However, by the 1920s the independence movement split into a conservative Islamic wing and a secular, even communist, wing. All forms of resistance (mostly non-violent) were suppressed by the Dutch.

The situation changed dramatically after the German occupation of Holland in 1940 and the Japanese occupation of the Dutch East Indies in 1941–42. A number of the leading figures of the independence movement collaborated with Japan in the hope of independence. As a result, Indonesia was spared the bloody clashes that occurred in the neighboring lands and the withdrawal of the Japanese in 1945 was a relatively controlled event.

With the help of the British, the Dutch tried to regain their control over the islands, but by the end of 1949 the former colonial power was defeated by independence fighters. However, the young state was faced with immediate internal threats. In western and central Java and on parts of Sumatra, conservative Muslims of the "Dar ul-Islam" movement began a struggle against the nationalist (and secular) government.

Their goal was to create a theocracy in Indonesia. It was not until 1962 that the movement was completely crushed by the central government, although the war cost thousands of lives.

Another trouble spot emerged in North Sumatra, in the realm of the former Sultanate of Aceh. Here, religiously inspired guerrillas had successfully resisted the Japanese occupation. By 1953, this movement had established ties with the "Dar ul-Islam." However, unlike the Dar ul-Islam, Jakarta could not completely subdue Acheh and so a compromise was reached, allowing for Acheh to officially retain much of its Islamic character. Nevertheless, fighting occasionally flared and it was only in the wake of the tsunami disaster of 2004 that a lasting peace treaty was agreed upon.

The Dutch were not the only colonial power to make its might felt in Southeast Asia. During the decades before and after the Napoleonic wars, the British began establishing power bases in what is now Malaysia and Borneo. One significant legacy of the British was the importation of large groups of Chinese and Indian merchants and laborers. By the time independence came in 1957, the indigenous Malays made up only 50 percent of the population. Considerable ethnic tensions ensued until the 1960s, when suitable agreements were put in place. Today, Malaysia (and neighboring Singapore) possesses a relatively stable government and vibrant economy.

Islam arrived in the Philippines via Indonesia. In 1475, the Sultanate of Sulu was established around the Islamized southern island of Mindanao. In 1571, the Spanish colonized the archipelago and eventually turned it into the only Christian-majority country in Asia. For centuries, Muslims of the southern islands resisted the colonialists.

After the end of Spanish rule over the Philippines in 1899, the Muslims continued their struggle for sovereignty, initially against the new colonial power—the United States—and later against the governments of the independent republic.

Muslims in China

Islam came to China by land and sea. By 758 CE there was already a Muslim community in the city of Canton made up primarily of merchants. Large parts of western China (today's Xinjiang Province) were inhabited almost exclusively by Muslim peoples, predominantly the Turkic Uyghurs. The Uyghurs had initially followed Buddhism, which found its way into Central and East Asia via the Silk Road from India. Christian teachings and the gnostic faith of Manichaeism became widespread here through the same route. Under the cultural influence of the Seljuks, Islam finally won a decisive influence from the eleventh and twelfth centuries onward.

In Gansu and other parts of the empire, Arab and Persian traders and mercenaries intermarried with local Han women and, as a result, the Hui people came into being. The Hui today form a so-called national minority and they have their own autonomous province of Ningxia that they have predominated since the Ming Dynasty (1368–1644).

Since 1785, the Muslim peoples of East Turkestan (Xinjiang) have repeatedly tried to resist Beijing, but in vain. In 1873, Yakub Beg took advantage of the massive civil turmoil in China to attempt to form a state, with the city of Kashgar as its capital. This attempt to grab freedom ended bloodily in 1878 and the Chinese government massacred hundreds of thousands of Muslim civilians. For a time, the region came back under Chinese control.

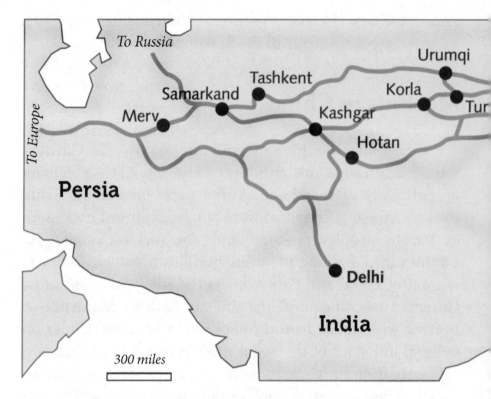

During the Chinese Civil War, the Muslims in western China actually succeeded in forming a republic in East Turkestan in 1944. However, it was destroyed by the new communist government under Mao Zedong in 1949. In its place came the "Uyghur Autonomous Province Xin Jiang" in 1955, although real autonomy for the Uyghur Muslims remained (and remains) very far out of reach.

During the period of the "Great Leap Forward" (1958–60), the Communist Party sought to eradicate the identities of China's minority populations. Islamic religious customs and the use of non-Han languages and writing were forbidden. With the calamitous failure of this experiment in social engineering in 1961, such restrictions were eased considerably.

The respite was short-lived, as the Cultural Revolution of 1965 aggravated the situation of China's Muslims again. Only the new constitution of 1982 gave minorities certain special

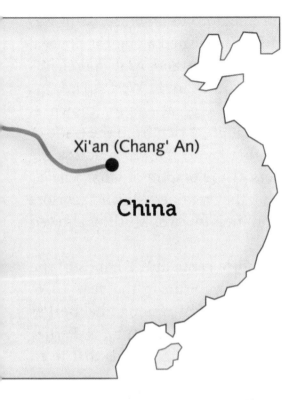

Xi'an (Chang' An)

China

rights—however—with limitations. Since then, a massive influx of Han Chinese into Eastern Turkestan has made the native Muslim Uyghurs a minority in their own homeland. Occasional acts of violence by Uyghur activists continue to be met with brutal reprisals and Beijing has implemented a number of regulations restricting the rights of the Muslim population of this area of China.

Islam in West Africa

Islam has had very early contacts with Africa. Ethiopia was, in fact, the first place of refuge for the nascent Muslim community of Mecca. Muslims began to filter through the vast Sahara Desert into West Africa as early as the eighth century CE. As commerce and trade had been exchanged between North Africa (and beyond) and Sub-Saharan Africa for centuries, it was only natural that ideas and religions would also be introduced. By the time the Murabitun of North Africa began to expand south to the Senegal River in the 1040s, Islam had already become a considerable influence in that part of West Africa.

The first known African kingdom to embrace Islam was the Kingdom of Takrur, which was located along the Senegal River. By the eleventh century, Berber and Arab merchants from Morocco helped the growth of Islam in West Africa.

A little south of Takrur was the great empire known as Ghana. It was a wealthy land that grew rich from the trade of salt and gold with the lands that lay to the north across the vast Sahara Desert. The rulers of the empire of Ghana never completely embraced Islam but they retained Muslim advisors and administrators. This friendliness towards Muslims allowed for Islam to further spread.

The end of the Ghana Empire came at the hands of the fundamentalist movement Al-Murabitun in the year 1076. The Murabitun movement had begun among the Berber tribes of North Africa. In the eleventh century, a Berber named Tarsina declared jihad against the pagans that lived along the Senegal River.

The fighting spread further south and soon the Ghana Empire came into conflict with the Murabitun. In 1062 the Murabitun declared war against Ghana and after nearly fourteen years of fighting, Ghana was destroyed. The fall of Ghana accelerated the spread of Islam in West Africa.

The empire of Mali rose from the ruins of the Ghana Empire. This state is important in the history of West Africa because it was the first great Islamic empire in the region. There are two main figures in the history of Mali whom we should know: Sundiata Keita (1190–1255) and Mansa Musa (who died in 1337).

Sundiata was the founder of the Mali Empire. Sundiata's life is shrouded in legend and his exploits form part of a great oral epic. By the time Sundiata died in 1255, a large part of West Africa had come under his power.

After Sundiata died, his two sons took over rule of the empire. They seem to not have left any remarkable achievements, but their nephew, Mansa Musa, came to be one of Africa's greatest kings. Raised in the company of Sunni Muslim scholars, Mansa Musa was a strict Muslim, unlike his predecessors. Mansa (a title which means "emperor") Musa took the throne of Mali in 1312 and his fame spread through Africa and the Middle East, and he even became known in Europe. During his twenty-five-year rule Mansa Musa made a pilgrimage to Makkah. He took with him his entire court, along with bodyguards. It is said he had so much gold with him that when he came through Cairo he disrupted the whole economy for years.

When he returned from his pilgrimage, Mansa Musa brought back to West Africa many Islamic scholars from Egypt and the Middle East. Many huge mosques were constructed throughout the realm and Islamic learning spread widely. Many of the pagan peoples that lived along the Niger River entered into Islam during the rule of Mansa Musa.

Mansa Musa's pilgrimage to Makkah was in many ways an advertisement of Mali's great wealth. This attracted hundreds of Muslim traders and scholars from the Middle East and North Africa. These individuals contributed to the cultural and economic development of the empire. Arabic became a widespread language and it helped unite the many different ethnic groups that made up the Mali Empire.

The last great African Islamic state was the Tokolor Sultanate, which at its height encompassed what is now much of Senegal, Guinea, and Mali. The state was founded by a remarkable man named Umar Taal. Born in the northern part of Senegal in 1797, Umar spent his youth studying Islam in the madrasahs of his region. At the age of twenty-three, Umar Tall made the Hajj and on his return he stayed as a respected guest of the Sultan of Sokoto. Umar Taal was also a Sufi shaykh.

In 1836, Umar Taal returned to the highlands along the Senegal River and for the next twelve years, he preached Islam to the non-Muslims of the area, calling on Muslims to revive their faith. Because of his great popularity, many of the local chiefs sought to weaken Umar Taal's influence, but they failed. In 1848, Umar Taal, along with several thousand of his followers, declared jihad against the polytheist chiefdoms that opposed the spread of Islam. He was successful and he began to form an Islamic state, with himself as head.

Umar Taal's conquests were halted by the French. Since the early nineteenth century the French and British had been making inroads into West Africa, at first making treaties with local rulers and then slowly exerting their political and military power. After Umar Taal's death in 1864, his son and his nephew continued to expand the state, but the power of the French military could not be stopped. In 1892, the Tokolor Sultanate fell, and along with it fell one of the last independent Islamic states in Africa.

By the 1890s the whole of West Africa was under the control of the French and British, with the French controlling the largest area of land. It was not until the 1950s and 1960s that most of these territories became independent states once again.

In the first decades of the twenty-first century, a group known as Boko Haram has caused considerable mayhem in northern Nigeria and in the surrounding countries. Unfortunately, the sad state of government in most sub-Saharan African countries has led to an inability to properly combat this growing problem.

The Modern Middle East

Since the end of World War II, four elements have defined the political visibility of Islam in this very important part of the world:

1. The continued dispute with Israel;
2. the establishment of Arab nationalist states;
3. the struggle over the strategically important oil resources; and
4. the Islamic revolution in Iran.

To this can be added a fifth element, one that has moved to the forefront since the 1990s, and that is the activity of the aggressive "Islamist" movements, which have now attained global reach.

The Suez Crisis

In the early 1950s Egypt assumed a leadership role in the quest for Arab unity. In July 1952, a military coup staged by leftist army officers overthrew King Farouk. Egypt's new leader, the famed Gamal Abd-el Nasser, enjoyed wide popularity not only within the country but internationally as well. In 1956, Nasser decided to nationalize the last bastion of European rule in the Middle East, the Suez Canal. Here, the British had stationed 80,000 soldiers, and roughly half of the strategic waterway's assets were in private French hands.

Simultaneously, Egypt approached the Soviet Union and its allies. This would set the trend for other revolutionary governments in the Muslim World (such as Libya, Syria, Iraq, and Indonesia) to seek help from the Communists. London and

Paris responded to the nationalization of the Suez Canal with violence. They included Israel in their planning; Israeli troops invaded the Gaza Strip and the Sinai Peninsula in late October 1956, driving back any Egyptian resistance. To "protect" the Suez Canal, British and French paratroopers began landing in the Northern Canal Zone and arrived at Port Said a few days later. The Europeans won a military victory, but they failed politically. The United Nations unanimously condemned actions taken by the aggressors, forcing them to withdraw.

Nasser worked to further his idea of a vast Arab Union. In 1958, Egypt merged with Syria to form the "United Arab Republic." It was a dream that would only last three years. Seeing the threat that the pro-Soviet socialist (and Marxist) regimes throughout the Arab world posed to their power, the monarchies of the Gulf began to forge closer ties to America and the West.

The Six-Day War

In November 1966 Egypt signed a military pact with Syria. Similar agreements were concluded with Jordan and Iraq in the late spring of 1967. At the same time, Cairo called on the United Nations to withdraw its peace-keeping troops stationed in the Gaza Strip and the Sinai Peninsula. Foreseeing these moves as signs of a looming attack, Israel struck at Egypt, Jordan, and Syria on June 4, 1967. On the first day the Israeli Air Force destroyed nearly all of the combat aircraft of the three Arab states. Within five days it succeeded in occupying the Gaza Strip, the Sinai Peninsula, the West Bank (including East Jerusalem), and Syria's Golan Heights. Egypt lost 11,500 soldiers and 80 percent of its military equipment, Jordan 6,000, and Syria at least 2,500.

Even more painful than the human and material loss was the humiliating defeat caused by a relatively small non-Muslim army on three Arab states.

Simultaneously, the Palestinian Liberation Organization (the PLO), whose goal was the liberation of Palestine, began to step up its covert war against Israel. Following the first Arab-Israeli War of 1948, nearly one million Palestinians were expelled from their homeland and forced to settle in refugee camps in Jordan, Syria, Lebanon, and elsewhere.

The October War

In September 1970, Egyptian President Nasser died. His successor, Anwar Sadat, moved away from the position of his predecessor by lessening Egypt's reliance on Soviet military aid. At the same time he intensified his aggressive rhetoric against Israel. On October 6, 1973, which was ten days into the month of Ramadan, over 30,000 Egyptian troops (with nearly half a million in reserve) crossed the Suez Canal, broke through the Israeli fortifications that lined the opposing bank, and began advancing into Sinai. Simultaneously, Syrian troops advanced against the Golan Heights, which had been occupied by Israel since the war of 1967. It seemed for a while that victory was in the Arabs' grasp, as the Israelis were totally unprepared for the attack.

However, massive arms shipments from the United States allowed the Israelis to counter-attack, and this led to a stalemate. On the Sinai front, the Egyptians were east of the Suez Canal in the northern sector, while in the southern sector Israeli units had crossed the Suez and occupied chunks of Egyptian territory. A ceasefire came into effect in late October 1973.

Even if the Arabs did not achieve their military goals, the hitherto strong Israeli psyche had been shaken. Nevertheless, the Egyptian President Sadat took the initiative to be the first Arab nation to reach a settlement with the Jewish state. In June 1975, the Suez Canal was reopened and a slow easing of tensions commenced on a number of levels. At the invitation of US President Jimmy Carter, Anwar Sadat and Israeli Prime Minister Menachem Begin accepted the Camp David Accords in September 1978, which led to the Egypt-Israel Peace Treaty being signed in early 1979.

At the outset, the separate peace with Israel caused Egypt to be isolated by other Arab states. Ultimately, in October 1981, President Sadat was assassinated in Cairo while observing a military parade. In the shadow of this Egyptian-Israeli rapprochement, two momentous conflicts broke out in the Islamic world: a civil war in Lebanon and a revolution in Iran.

Civil War in Lebanon

In the early 1970s, the flimsy balance of power between Maronite Christians and Muslims in Lebanon fell apart. The growing Muslim component of the population (bolstered by the mass migration of Palestinian refugees) had tilted the balance against the Maronites, and the once-dominant community feared for their supremacy in both politics and the economy. When Christian militiamen took action against Palestinian refugees living in southern Beirut in April 1975, open conflict broke out between Christians, Muslims, and Druze.

Muslims—both Sunnis and Shiites—generally expressed their solidarity with the Palestinians. This made the Christians even more aggressive and in the summer of 1976 Syria intervened in Lebanon on the side of the Sunnis.

Given that the PLO used southern Lebanon as a platform for repeatedly launching strikes against Israel, the Jewish state took advantage of the intensifying civil strife in Lebanon to hit back at its longtime foe—at first moderately, but by June 1982, massively. The Israeli army penetrated into Lebanon all the way to Beirut, forcing the leadership of the PLO to withdraw from Lebanon. It was at this time that

perhaps the greatest atrocity of the civil war occurred. With the tacit approval of the Israeli army, Christian militiamen entered two Palestinian refugee camps and slaughtered upwards of 2,000 unarmed civilians. Worldwide protests eventually pressured Israel to withdraw from Lebanon. A twenty-kilometer deep "security zone" was established by Israel in southern Lebanon, controlled by Lebanese Christians, to serve as a buffer between Israel and Palestinian guerrillas and the rising power of the Shiite Hezbollah. The fighting in the rest of Lebanon, however, went on unabated. Finally in 1989, a peace agreement was reached between the warring factions, although the Syrian military presence ended only in 2005. The civil war claimed more than 150,000 lives and ruined Lebanon politically and economically.

The Revolution in Iran

In the late 1970s a prolonged crisis of global proportions occurred in Iran with the so-called "Islamic Revolution." The causes of this revolution are deep and complicated. As early as 1905, the bourgeoisie and the clergy began demanding the establishment of a parliamentary system. The reigning monarch, Muzaffaruddin Qajar (d.1907), agreed to the formation of a constitutional monarchy; however, this was undone by his successor, Mohammad Ali Shah, who abolished the constitution and dissolved parliament. Pro-constitution forces rebelled and the country was thrown into turmoil. This encouraged the de facto partition of Persia (as Iran was known then) into Russian and British spheres of influence.

With the backing of the British, a Persian cavalry officer named Reza Khan seized control of the government in 1921, and in 1925 he drove the last monarch of the Qajar Dynasty from the throne, proclaiming himself the first shah of the Pahlavi Dynasty. Despite the opposition of the clergy and the traditionalists, Reza Shah forced a program of Westernization on Iranian society. A civil code came into force, displacing the traditional legal system based in the Shari'ah and religious schools were closed down. Women were strongly encouraged to don Western fashions, and the face veil was banned. Because of Reza Shah's pro-German stance during World War II, the British and Soviets invaded Iran in August 1941 and forced the Pahlavi ruler to abdicate in favor of his son, Mohammad Reza Shah.

Mohammad Reza Shah furthered the drastic modernization policies, and focused the nation on its pre-Islamic past, which of course angered religious conservatives. To this was added another crisis: In 1951 Muhammad Mossadeq, the pro-democracy Iranian prime minister, nationalized Iran's oil industry. This horrified the British and Americans, given that their companies owned most of this oil industry. In 1953 the CIA and SAS staged a coup that overthrew Mossadeq and reinstalled the Shah's regime. This was done partially out of a desire to regain control of Iran's oil industry and also the fear that Mossadeq's liberal political thinking would have eventually placed the country in the Soviet camp. However, the overthrow of a democratically elected government angered many, and would not be forgotten.

With solid support from America, Mohammad Reza Shah embarked on an extensive modernization program in the 1960s. In 1965, for instance, there were only 694 factories in the country, but this number rose to 5,661 by 1972. The life expectancy also increased drastically with the opening of modern hospitals and clinics. At the same time, the gap dividing rich and poor, urban and rural, widened. This fact, plus the dynasty's continued de-emphasis of Iran's Islamic heritage, added much to the growing popular discontent with the Shah.

A number of political demonstrations were bloodily suppressed in 1978, and a wave of strikes swept the country. As the intensity of the upheaval grew, the Shah and his family fled the country. For the first time in 2,500 years of history, Iran was without a monarch.

Although a number of resistance groups played a role in the revolution, the primary force behind the Shah's overthrow was the Shiite clergy, represented by the Ayatollah Khomeini, who had been in exile since 1964. Khomeini returned to Iran in February 1979 and on April 1, the Islamic Republic of Iran was proclaimed, with Khomeini at its head. Western clothes became frowned upon, women had to cover their heads, and the separation of the sexes in public was supervised by morals policing. With the assumption of power by the clergy, the foreign policy of Iran made an about-face. Although America had been Iran's close ally since the 1953 coup, it was now branded the "Great Satan." In late November 1979, a mob of university students seized the American embassy in Tehran and took the staff hostage in response to the United States admitting the Shah into the country for medical treatment. Despite various efforts to free the American hostages (including a failed military mission) they would remain in captivity for fourteen months.

In the exuberance of their successful revolution, the Iranian government and clergy began to "export" their revolution to other Muslim countries—especially those with Shiite populations. Neighboring Iraq was particularly disturbed by this action. Since the overthrow of the monarchy in 1958, the Iraqi government emphasized secularism, socialism, and uncompromising Arab nationalism. The Shiite majority (which was the target of Iran's exported revolution) of Iraq was dominated by a Sunni minority, to which dictator Saddam Hussein belonged. There had been in the past repeated border disputes between Iraq and Iran, especially over the far southwestern corner of Iran which was home to an ethnic Arab minority and—conveniently—most of Iran's oil reserves.

Given that the regular armed forces of Iran were in organizational disarray owing to the revolution, the Iraqis took advantage of this and invaded Iran in September 1980. After initial successes, their advance was checked by the Iranians and by June 1982 Iraqi troops had retreated behind international borders. The regime of the newly established Islamic Republic now sought to liberate the sacred Shi'i sites located inside of Iraq. The bloody trench warfare dragged on until battlefield deaths surged upwards of a million lives. Yet, Iraq remained a security risk in the region. The country had already tried to compel "unification" with the neighboring sheikdom Kuwait in 1961 and 1973. In August 1990, Saddam's army invaded its small neighbor and occupied it. Most Arab states expressed solidarity with Kuwait and sent symbolic military contingents troops to bolster Saudi Arabia's defenses. Simultaneously, the United States and the West put their military machine in motion and they drove the Iraqis out of Kuwait in January 1991. However, the Allies did not entirely destroy Saddam's regime; in fact, they left him with enough strength to brutally crush an uprising by Iraq's ethnic Kurdish (who were mainly Sunni) and Shi'ah populations in front of the eyes of the world. Saddam made sure that he remained in office unchallenged.

The Palestinian-Israeli Conflict

A traffic accident in the Gaza Strip in which an Israeli truck driver killed four Palestinians in December 1987, sparked what came to be known as the First Intifada. This was a year-long popular uprising of mostly young Palestinians, who attacked (primarily by stone throwing) Israeli soldiers and settlers in the occupied territories; at its end more than 300 Palestinians had been killed by Israeli security forces.

However, the collapse of the Soviet Bloc in the late 1980s altered the situation between the Palestinians and the Israelis. Gradually, the PLO and the Jewish state took steps to come to some form of understanding. In October 1991, official high-level talks between the two sides were held in Madrid. Israeli Prime Minister Shamir and the Foreign Ministers of Syria, Lebanon, and Jordan, and PLO representatives sat at the negotiating table, but without substantial results.

Following secret talks in Norway in 1994, Israel endorsed, among other things, Palestinian self-government in the Gaza Strip and in the city of Jericho. However, a number of issues remained unresolved, such as the size of the areas under question and the control of the borders of the autonomous areas.

Yet peace remained elusive. In February 1994, an Israeli settler killed 29 Palestinians and injured 125 more in an attack on a mosque. Forty days later, eight Israelis in northern Israel were killed in attacks carried out by Hamas, a Palestinian Islamist organization.

Towards the end of that year, the PLO and Israel agreed, among other things, to normalize diplomatic relations with each other and Israel agreed to return land to Jordan. In 1995, a further agreement called for the gradual withdrawal of Israeli troops from the major cities of the West Bank. However, conservative opposition to this plan was strong in Israel and at a rally in Tel Aviv in November 1995, Prime Minister Yitzhak Rabin (who spearheaded the Israeli side of the negotiations) was assassinated by a right-wing Jewish extremist. The murder shocked both Israelis and Palestinians alike.

The new Prime Minister, the right-wing Benjamin Netanyahu, an outspoken opponent of the agreements, initially froze all contact with the Palestinians. Despite the significant deterioration in Israeli-Palestinian relations, Netanyahu and Arafat finally agreed in January 1997 on a compromise formula with regard to the conflict over the city of Hebron/Khalil. This city continues to be of high symbolic value for Jews, Christians, and Muslims, for here—according to tradition—lay the tombs of Abraham, Isaac, and Jacob. For centuries, a mosque has encircled these tombs. Hebron has a population that is overwhelmingly Palestinian, with only 500 Jews living in the city center. To protect these militant settlers, up to 2,000 Israeli soldiers are stationed in Hebron. Despite their numbers, the Palestinians living here continue to be subjected to considerable restrictions.

The situation regarding the city of Jerusalem remains perpetually complicated. The Israelis consider this city (which they seized in its entirety in 1967) as the capital of their state. The Palestinians likewise claim Jerusalem as the capital of any future independent state they may form. Both parties view their claims to the city as non-negotiable and it remains a point of contention that blocks any comprehensive peace plan. As of 2011, the population of Jerusalem is approximately 62 percent Jewish, 35 percent Muslim, and 2 percent Christian.

Throughout the first decade of the twenty-first century, the conservative government of Israel never completely ceased peace talks, despite many setbacks. Covert diplomacy continued to be carried out. In October 1998, a memorandum was agreed upon by both parties for the further implementation of the 1994 Gaza-Jericho Agreement. However, in September 2000, the then-opposition leader Ariel Sharon's "visit" to the Temple Mount sparked a Second Intifada, which triggered a new and seemingly enduring revolt against Israeli occupation forces. The Intifada and its attempted suppression overturned, or seriously hindered, any of the agreements that were on the table, or even those yet to come. Since the 2000 Intifada, Israel has disrupted nearly all attempts by the Palestinians to form an infrastructure for a state. Israel began the construction of a massive wall that further fragmented the Palestinian areas of the West Bank, rendering an independent and viable Palestinian state illusory. The conservative government of Israel continues to this day to allow substantial Jewish settlements to be built in the West Bank, despite it being a clear violation of agreements as well as international law.

The position of the Palestinian Islamist movements, like Hamas and the Islamic Jihad Movement (IJM), has further complicated negotiations. Rising out of relative obscurity during the 1980s, these organizations were able to capitalize on the failures of the secular PLO to secure favorable terms with the Israelis. The hardline approach of such groups in dealing with the Jewish state, high unemployment, and the lack of any future prospects solidifies the negative attitude of most Palestinians against the State of Israel and ensures a constant support base for Islamic militants—disenchanted and demoralized young people who do not shy away from suicide bombings. Under the current conditions, further reconciliation between Israelis and Palestinians has become almost unattainable.

A resolution to this conflict is long overdue in order to have peace and harmony in the region and the world. The United Nations and world powers need to deal with both countries equally and justly, and reinforce the two-state solution according to the UN resolutions.

Endless War in Afghanistan

In the shadow of the Middle Eastern conflict, a civil war in Afghanistan in 1978 soon turned into an international conflict. Afghanistan has been an ethnically and politically unstable country from time immemorial. Throughout its history, its numerous ethnic groups vied for power and then later both the British and Russians fought for influence over the land. In 1973, the last monarch was overthrown and the country was proclaimed a republic. A coup by pro-Soviet army officers in 1978 brought about the Democratic Republic of Afghanistan, but the new government had to deal with opposition from the mostly conservative provincial and tribal leaders. The Soviets grew alarmed because this Islamic resistance threatened to destabilize the situation on its southern borders, more so since the Islamic revolution in neighboring Iran was occurring at the same time.

In December 1979, the Soviets decided to intervene to help their pro-Soviet regime against the anti-communist rebels. By 1983, the number of Soviet troops stationed in Afghanistan grew to 90,000. Against this invasion by the Soviet Union, a coalition was formed, one that came to be called the Mujahidin, or "Those who wage jihad." Pakistan and Iran helped the Mujahidin logistically, while the Saudis and Americans supplied them with money and weaponry. The Mujahidin also attracted Islamist fighters from the Arab world, who traveled to Afghanistan in order to support its native people in the fight against the "godless infidels."

Initially, the government forces and the Red Army were able to retain control of the few urban centers in the country. However, in 1984–85, the Russians went on the offensive in Afghanistan with 115,000 soldiers. Meanwhile, the reform-minded Mikhail Gorbachev came to power in the Soviet Union. He was prepared to slowly defuse the conflict, seeing its extensive drain on the Soviet economy. Nevertheless, the US and Saudi Arabia continued to massively support the opposition. By 1987, Washington alone had sent nearly $700 million to the Mujahidin groups, a number of whom were as anti-Western as they were anti-Soviet.

In May 1988, the Soviets finally began the withdrawal of their troops, which was completed in February 1989. They had lost some 14,000 soldiers in the decade of violence, compared to some 75,000 Mujahidin. However, the civilian population suffered horribly: one to one and a half million Afghans perished during the war, and approximately six million people were made refugees.

After the Russian withdrawal, war broke out between the former Mujahidin coalition partners in a struggle for power in the newly liberated country. Numerous regional warlords began emerging throughout the land and Afghanistan simply fell into further chaos. The ongoing fighting ruined the relatively modern and previously intact capital of Kabul.

Therefore, at first, the Afghan population, weary of chaos and war, welcomed the intervention of the Taliban, the so-called "religious students" militiamen. The Taliban seized Kandahar in 1994 and a year later the ruins of Kabul. The feuding Mujahidin groups were no match for them and with widespread support the Taliban were able to take hold of large swaths of the country.

Once in power, the Taliban established a puritanical theocracy along the lines of Saudi Arabia. Women, for instance, were wholly excluded from public life, and they were not allowed to work. What was left of the educational and healthcare systems collapsed. Music and other forms of entertainment were henceforth forbidden, all men were required to grow beards, and public executions were regular occurrences.

For years the world took little notice of the Taliban. It was not until September 11, 2001—when two hijacked passenger planes brought down the World Trade Center in New York—that Afghanistan moved back into focus. This was because a certain Osama Bin Laden had resided there since the days of the anti-Soviet struggle.

The scion of a wealthy Saudi family, Osama Bin Laden was identified as the mastermind behind the September 11, 2001 attacks on the United States. The United States and its allies took military action against the Taliban regime, and a pro-Western regime was installed. Yet, despite their losses, the Taliban continues to fight against the United States and its Afghan allies, utilizing the rugged mountainous terrain to their advantage.

The Overthrow of Saddam's Iraq

In March 2003 American and Allied armies swept aside the Iraqi dictatorship of Saddam Hussein in a mere three weeks. While the Iraqi people were freed from an oppressive and heartless regime, at the same time the country descended into an unprecedented wave of chaos and terror. Sectarian and ethnic conflict—which had been contained by Saddam's brutality—broke out all over the land. The long-suppressed Shi'ite majority began to exert itself (much to the delight of neighboring Iran), much to the resentment of the once ruling Sunni minority. The Kurds (a people who are primarily Sunni, but racially distinct from Arabs) began to clamor for self-rule over the lands they populated in the north and northeastern parts of Iraq. Governmental stability and law and order were only precariously maintained, until the blitzkrieg by ISIS (the so-called "Islamic State of Iraq and Syria") plunged Iraq into further turmoil. This was the beginning of the "Arab Spring" and the rise of ISIS.

In December 2010 a series of protests, riots, and revolutions broke out in the Arab world, which were triggered by an anti-government uprising in Tunisia. These disturbances gradually spread to several countries in the Arab Middle East and North Africa, their target being the authoritarian ruling regimes, and the oppressive political structures and failed economies of these countries.

These popular uprisings managed to topple long-time dictators, such as Egypt's Hosni Mubarak, Libya's Muammar Qaddafi, and Yemen's Ali Abdullah Saleh. While there was the hope of democratic change, these countries soon devolved into further violent bedlam. Egypt fell back under military rule, and Libya and Yemen fell into civil war, which, as of the writing of this book, are ongoing.

Yet, the bloodiest and most menacing of these popular uprisings is the one that took place in Syria. This country had long been governed by the Assad family, whose rule was typical of the other military dictatorships that were so common throughout the Arab world. Their rule also contained a sectarian dimension, given that the Assads were members of a small Shi'ite sect (known as the Alawites). ISIS represents a toxic mix of religious ideology and the political chaos that has afflicted the Middle East for the last century. In the spring of 2011, peaceful protests were held in a number of Syrian towns and cities. The government responded with violence and soon the entire country was in flames.

While the initial fighting between the opposition and government forces was more political in character, as the violence intensified so did the sectarian aspect of the conflict. Iran directly supported the Assad regime, as did the Lebanese Shi'ite militia Hezbollah. The Sunni states of the Gulf and Turkey supplied and supported the opposition. World powers also became party to this conflict, with Russia supporting the Assad regime while the Unites States of America supported the anti-Assad regime. Islamist groups—with nearly two decades of experience of guerrilla combat in Afghanistan, Chechnya, Bosnia, and elsewhere—also saw the pandemonium in Syria as a chance to extend their power and influence. ISIS is one of the groups that thrust itself to the fore. As of the writing of this book, the multi-factional battle for Syria and Iraq continues to rage with no end in sight.

It is to be noted that during this five-year war in Syria, a quarter of a million people (mostly Muslims) have lost their lives. Over 13.5 million (mostly Muslims) have left their homes, 6.5 million people (mostly Muslims) have been displaced within Syria, and another 4.4 million (mostly Muslims) have fled the country as refugees, prompting the world's worst refugee crisis since World War II. We have seen disturbing images of dead

Syrian children washed up on European beaches and wounded and shocked children in ambulances.

Refugee Crisis

According to the recent figures by the Internal Displacement Monitoring Centre (IDMC), more than 40.8 million people around the world are internally displaced. This displacement is due to the conflicts, violence, wars, drought, disease outbreaks or natural disasters.

Beside the human displacement crisis, there is another crisis called refugee crisis. A refugee is a person who has been forced to leave their country (cross the internationally recognized border) in order to escape war, persecution, or natural disaster. In Syria alone, an estimated 11 million people have fled their homes since the outbreak of the civil war in March 2011. Among those escaping the conflict, the majority have sought refuge in neighboring countries or within Syria itself. In Syria, over a quarter of a million people (mostly Muslims) lost their lives. Over 13.5 million (mostly Muslims) are in need of humanitarian assistance; 6.6 million people (mostly Muslims) had been displaced within Syria; another 5 million (mostly Muslims) had fled the country as refugees, prompting the world's worst refugee crisis since the 2nd World War. More than 4.8 million Syrian refugees are in just five countries Turkey, Lebanon, Jordan, Iraq and Egypt. We have seen the disturbing images of the dead Syrian children floating to the European beaches and wounded and shocked children in the ambulances.

There are other refugee crisis as well like Rohingya Muslim refugees Crisis in Myanmar, the African refugee Crisis (Nigeria, Republic of Congo, Sudan, Libya, Somalia, Sudan, Cameron and Ethiopia, etc.) and many other countries and most of them have dense Muslim population.

We hope and pray for the peace and prosperity in our global village.

Conclusion

What can be garnered from this very brief outline of the political performance of more than 1,300 years of Muslim history is sobering and it does not differ from the history of other parts of the world. It is the same constant recurrence of war and violence, oppression and exploitation, as can be found in Europe, America, or in East Asia. Thus, Muslims are no more objectionable or wholesome than any other set of human beings.

Currently, the vast majority of Muslim states are governed either by single party dictatorships, feudal despots, or inflexible religious zealots. Yet, we have in the last few years witnessed the chaos that is unleashed when such rulers are brought down. Obviously, such political and social subjugation has no doubt played a very major role in the inertia, stagnation, and hopelessness found over a wide swath of the Muslim world. The negative influence of meddling and intervening outside forces cannot be minimized either.

While a comprehensive investigation of the 150-year-long crisis that the Muslim world continues to face is beyond the scope of this small book, it is hoped that the readers may use the basic information presented here as a springboard for further investigation, and that whatever conclusions are drawn from this reading will broaden an understanding of Islam, of Muslims, and of the violence perpetrated in the name of one of the world's greatest religious traditions.

We, the citizens of this global village, have the opportunity to make history where Jews, Christians, Muslims, and people of other faiths and no faith can live side by side as one big human family with cooperation, mutual respect, peace, harmony, and prosperity.

Islam presents the diversity of skin colors and languages as signs from God [Qur'an 30:22] and promotes human dignity [Qur'an 17:70], justice [Qur'an 16:90], equality [Qur'an 49:13] and liberty [Qur'an 2:256], which are also guaranteed by the constitution of the United States of America.

Appendices

Qur'anic References

Please note that first number is in reference to the Surah (chapter) and the second number after the colon represents the Ayah (verse of that chapter). This translation is by Sahih International and can be obtained at http://www.quran.com.

Qur'an, 33:56 (Recommendation for sending salutation to the Prophet Muhammad, peace and blessings be upon him)
Surely Allah and His angels bless the Prophet; O you who believe! Call for (Divine) blessings on him and salute him with a (becoming) salutation.

Qur'an, 112:1–4 (Who is God?)
Say: He, Allah, is One. Allah is He on Whom all depend. He begets not, nor is He begotten. And none is like Him.

Qur'an, 42:11 (Who is God?)
The Originator of the heavens and the earth; He made mates for you from among yourselves, and mates of the cattle too, multiplying you thereby; nothing like a likeness of Him; and He is the Hearing, the Seeing.

Qur'an, 50:16 (Where is God?)
And We have already created man and know what his soul whispers to him, and We are closer to him than [his] jugular vein.

Qur'an, 66:06 (Angels don't disobey God)
O you who have believed, protect yourselves and your families from a Fire whose fuel is people and stones, over which are [appointed] angels, harsh and severe; they do not disobey Allah in what He commands them but do what they are commanded.

Qur'an, 33:40 (Muhammad is the final messenger)
Muhammad is not the father of [any] one of your men, but [he is] the Messenger of Allah and last of the prophets. And ever is Allah, of all things, Knowing.

Qur'an, 98:02 (The message and the messenger)
A Messenger from Allah, reciting purified scriptures.

Qur'an, 75:6–14 (The Last Day)
He asks, "When is the Day of Resurrection?" So when vision is dazzled, And the moon darkens, and the sun and the moon are joined. Man will say on that Day, "Where is the [place of] escape?" No! There is no refuge. To your Lord, that Day, is the [place of] permanence. Man will be informed that Day of what he sent ahead and kept back. Rather, man, against himself, will be a witness.

Qur'an, 57:22 (Good or bad decreed by God)
No disaster strikes upon the earth or among yourselves except that it is in a register before We bring it into being—indeed that, for Allah, is easy.

Qur'an, 51:56 (Acts of worship)
And I did not create the jinn and mankind except to worship Me.

Qur'an, 25:70 (Profession of faith and repentance)
Except for those who repent, believe and do righteous work. For them Allah will replace their evil deeds with good. And ever is Allah Forgiving and Merciful.

Qur'an, 2:3 (Daily prayers)
Who believe in the unseen, establish prayer, and spend out of what We have provided for them.

Qur'an, 17:78 (Daily prayer timings)
Establish prayer at the decline of the sun [from its meridian] until the darkness of the night and [also] the Qur'an of dawn. Indeed, the recitation of dawn is ever witnessed.

Qur'an, 4:103 (Regulated timing for prayer)
And when you have completed the prayer, remember Allah standing, sitting, or [lying] on your sides. But when you become secure, re-establish [regular] prayer. Indeed, prayer has been decreed upon the believers a decree of specified times.

Qur'an, 5:6 (Ablution is called Wudu)
O you who have believed, when you rise to [perform] prayer, wash your faces and your forearms to the elbows and wipe over your heads and wash your feet to the ankles. And if you are in a state of janabah, then purify yourselves. But if you are ill or on a journey or one of you comes from the place of relieving himself or you have contacted women and do not find water, then seek clean earth and wipe over your faces and hands with it. Allah does not intend to make difficulty for you, but He intends to purify you and complete His favor upon you that you may be grateful.

Qur'an, 62:9 (Friday prayer)
O you who have believed, when [the adhan] is called for the prayer on the day of Jumu'ah [Friday], then proceed to the remembrance of Allah and leave trade. That is better for you, if you only knew.

Qur'an, 2:184 (Exceptions from fasting)

[Fasting for] a limited number of days. So whoever among you is ill or on a journey [during them]—then an equal number of days [are to be made up]. And upon those who are able [to fast, but with hardship]—a ransom [as substitute] of feeding a poor person [each day]. And whoever volunteers excess—it is better for him. But to fast is best for you, if you only knew.

Qur'an, 2:185 (Significance of Ramadan)

The month of Ramadan [is that] in which was revealed the Qur'an, a guidance for the people and clear proof of guidance and criterion. So whoever sights [the new moon of] the month, let him fast it, and whoever is ill or on a journey—then an equal number of other days. Allah intends for you ease and does not intend for you hardship and [wants] for you to complete the period and to glorify Allah for that [to] which He has guided you; and perhaps you will be grateful.

Qur'an, 2:183 (Prescription of fasting)

O you who have believed, decreed upon you is fasting as it was decreed upon those before you that you may become righteous

Qur'an, 2:185 (Ending Ramadan)

The month of Ramadan [is that] in which was revealed the Qur'an, a guidance for the people and clear proof of guidance and criterion. So whoever sights [the new moon of] the month, let him fast it; and whoever is ill or on a journey—then an equal number of other days. Allah intends for you ease and does not intend for you hardship and [wants] for you to complete the period and to glorify Allah for that [to] which He has guided you; and perhaps you will be grateful.

Qur'an, 9:60 (Zakah distribution)

Zakah expenditures are only for the poor and for the needy and for those employed to collect [zakah] and for bringing hearts together [for Islam] and for freeing captives [or slaves] and for those in debt and for the cause of Allah and for the [stranded] traveler—an obligation [imposed] by Allah. And Allah is Knowing and Wise.

Qur'an, 2:127 (Rebuilding the Ka'bah)

And [mention] when Abraham was raising the foundations of the House and [with him] Ishmael, [saying], "Our Lord, accept [this] from us. Indeed You are the Hearing, the Knowing."

Qur'an, 3: 97 (Pilgrimage to Mecca)

In it are clear signs [such as] the standing place of Abraham. And whoever enters it shall be safe. And [due] to Allah from the people is a pilgrimage to the House—for whoever is able to find thereto a way. But whoever disbelieves—then indeed, Allah is free from need of the worlds.

Qur'an, 2:197 (Hajj details)

Hajj is [during] well-known months, so whoever has made Hajj obligatory upon himself therein [by entering the state of ihram], there is [to be for him] no sexual relations and no disobedience and no disputing during Hajj. And whatever good you do—Allah knows it. And take provisions, but indeed, the best provision is fear of Allah. And fear Me, O you of understanding.

Qur'an, 2:158 (Mount Safa and Marwah)

Indeed, as-Safa and al-Marwah are among the symbols of Allah. So whoever makes Hajj to the House or performs 'umrah—there is no blame upon him for walking between them. And whoever volunteers good—then indeed, Allah is appreciative and knowing.

Qur'an, 22:36–37 (Eid al-Adha)
And the camels and cattle We have appointed for you as among the symbols of Allah; for you therein is good. So mention the name of Allah upon them when lined up [for sacrifice]; and when they are [lifeless] on their sides, then eat from them and feed the needy and the beggar. Thus have We subjected them to you that you may be grateful. Their meat will not reach Allah, nor will their blood, but what reaches Him is piety from you. Thus We have subjected them to you that you may glorify Allah for that [to] which He has guided you; and give good tidings to the doers of good.

Qur'an, 15:9 (Preservation and protection of the Qur'an is upon God)
Indeed, it is We who sent down the Qur'an and indeed, We will be its guardian.

Qur'an, 4:80 (Status of the Prophet)
He who obeys the Messenger has obeyed Allah; but those who turn away—We have not sent you over them as a guardian.

Qur'an, 33:21 (The Prophet Muhammad as the best role model)
There has certainly been for you in the Messenger of Allah an excellent pattern for anyone whose hope is in Allah and the Last Day and [who] remembers Allah often.

Qur'an, 68:4 (Character of the Prophet)
And indeed, you are of a great moral character.

Qur'an, 3:31–32 (Condition to earn the love of God)

Say, [O Muhammad], "If you should love Allah, then follow me, [so] Allah will love you and forgive you your sins. And Allah is Forgiving and Merciful." Say: "Obey Allah and the Messenger." But if they turn away—then indeed, Allah does not like the disbelievers.

Qur'an, 6:145 (Prohibited food)

Say, "I do not find within that which was revealed to me [anything] forbidden to one who would eat it unless it be a dead animal or blood spilled out or the flesh of swine—for indeed, it is impure—or it be [that slaughtered in] disobedience, dedicated to other than Allah. But whoever is forced [by necessity], neither desiring [it] nor transgressing [its limit], then indeed, your Lord is Forgiving and Merciful."

Qur'an, 6:151–152 (Prohibited deeds)

Say, "Come, I will recite what your Lord has prohibited to you. [He commands] that you not associate anything with Him, and to parents, good treatment, and do not kill your children out of poverty; We will provide for you and them. And do not approach immoralities—what is apparent of them and what is concealed. And do not kill the soul which Allah has forbidden [to be killed] except by [legal] right. This has He instructed you that you may use reason." And do not approach the orphan's property except in a way that is best until he reaches maturity. And give full measure and weight in justice. We do not charge any soul except [with that within] its capacity. And when you testify, be just, even if [it concerns] a near relative. And the covenant of Allah is fulfilled. This has He instructed you that you may remember.

Qur'an, 5:90–91 (Deeds of Shaitan/Satan)

O you who have believed, indeed, intoxicants, gambling, [sacrificing on] stone alters [to other than Allah], and divining arrows are but defilement from the work of Satan, so avoid it that you may be successful. Satan only wants to cause between you animosity and hatred through intoxicants and gambling and to avert you from the remembrance of Allah and from prayer. So will you not desist?

Qur'an, 3:130 (Prohibited sources of income)

O you who have believed, do not consume usury, doubled and multiplied, but fear Allah that you may be successful.

Qur'an, 2:188 (Prohibited sources of income)

And do not consume one another's wealth unjustly or send it [in bribery] to the rulers in order that [they might aid] you [to] consume a portion of the wealth of the people in sin, while you know [it is unlawful].

Qur'an, 5:8 (Islam promotes justice even in favor of enemies)

O you who have believed, be persistently standing firm for Allah, witnesses in justice, and do not let the hatred of a people prevent you from being just. Be just; that is nearer to righteousness. And fear Allah; indeed, Allah is acquainted with what you do.

Qur'an, 4:135 (Islam promotes justice even against loved ones)

O you who have believed, be persistently standing firm in justice, witnesses for Allah, even if it be against yourselves or parents and relatives. Whether one is rich or poor, Allah is more worthy of both. So follow not [personal] inclination, lest you not be just. And if you distort [your testimony] or refuse [to give it], then indeed Allah is ever, with what you do, acquainted.

Qur'an, 49:13 (Equality)
O mankind, indeed We have created you from male and female and made you peoples and tribes that you may know one another. Indeed, the most noble of you in the sight of Allah is the most righteous of you. Indeed, Allah is Knowing and Acquainted.

Qur'an, 2:256 (Liberty)
There shall be no compulsion in [acceptance of] the religion. The right course has become clear from the wrong. So whoever disbelieves in Taghut (false deities and evil) and believes in Allah has grasped the most trustworthy handhold with no break in it. And Allah is Hearing and Knowing.

Qur'an, 17:70 (Dignity and honor for humans)
And We have certainly honored the children of Adam and carried them on the land and sea and provided for them of the good things and preferred them over much of what We have created, with [definite] preference.

Qur'an, 17:37 (Humility)
And do not walk upon the earth exultantly. Indeed, you will never tear the earth [apart], and you will never reach the mountains in height.

Qur'an, 39:53-54 (Hope in the mercy of God)
Say, "O My servants who have transgressed against themselves [by sinning], do not despair of the mercy of Allah. Indeed, Allah forgives all sins. Indeed, it is He who is the Forgiving, the Merciful." And return [in repentance] to your Lord and

submit to Him before the punishment comes upon you; then you will not be helped.

Qur'an, 49:11–12 (Forbidden attitudes)
O you who have believed, let not a people ridicule [another] people; perhaps they may be better than them; nor let women ridicule [other] women; perhaps they may be better than them. And do not insult one another and do not call each other by [offensive] nicknames. Wretched is the name of disobedience after [one's] faith. And whoever does not repent—then it is those who are the wrongdoers. O you who have believed, avoid much [negative] assumption. Indeed, some assumption is sin. And do not spy or backbite each other. Would one of you like to eat the flesh of his brother when dead? You would detest it. And fear Allah; indeed, Allah is Accepting of repentance and Merciful.

Qur'an, 49:13 (Humanity is one family)
O mankind, indeed We have created you from male and female and made you peoples and tribes that you may know one another. Indeed, the most noble of you in the sight of Allah is the most righteous of you. Indeed, Allah is Knowing and Acquainted.

Qur'an, 42:13 (Shari'ah is not new)
He has ordained for you of religion what He enjoined upon Noah and that which We have revealed to you, [O Muhammad], and what We enjoined upon Abraham and Moses and Jesus— to establish the religion and not be divided therein. Difficult for those who associate others with Allah is that to which you invite them. Allah chooses for Himself whom He wills and guides to Himself whoever turns back [to Him].

Qur'an, 45:18 (Shari'ah)

Then We put you, [O Muhammad], on an ordained way concerning the matter [of religion]; so follow it and do not follow the inclinations of those who do not know.

Qur'an, 42:49–50 (Gender)

To Allah belongs the dominion of the heavens and the earth; He creates what he wills. He gives to whom He wills female [children], and He gives to whom He wills males. Or He makes them [both] males and females, and He renders whom He wills barren. Indeed, He is Knowing and Competent.

Qur'an, 49:13 (Humanity is created from male and female)

O mankind, indeed We have created you from male and female and made you peoples and tribes that you may know one another. Indeed, the most noble of you in the sight of Allah is the most righteous of you. Indeed, Allah is Knowing and Acquainted.

Qur'an, 7:22–23 (Women are not singled out for eating from the forbidden tree)

So he (Satan) made (both of) them fall, through deception. And when they (both) tasted of the tree, their private parts became apparent to them (both), and they began to fasten together over themselves from the leaves of Paradise. And their Lord called to them (both), "Did I not forbid you (both) from that tree and tell you (both) that Satan is to you a clear enemy?" They (both) said, "Our Lord, we have wronged ourselves, and if You do not forgive us and have mercy upon us, we will surely be among the losers."

Qur'an, 4:124 (Gender equality in practice and rewards)
And whoever does righteous deeds, whether male or female, while being a believer—those will enter Paradise and will not be wronged, [even as much as] the speck on a date seed.

Qur'an, 30:21 (Purpose of marriage)
And of His signs is that He created for you from yourselves mates that you may find tranquility in them; and He placed between you affection and mercy. Indeed in that are signs for a people who give thought.

Qur'an, 4:3 (Polygamy)
And if you fear that you will not deal justly with the orphan girls, then marry those that please you of [other] women, two or three or four. But if you fear that you will not be just, then [marry only] one or those your right hand possesses. That is more suitable that you may not incline [to injustice].

Qur'an, 29:69 (Jihad against temptations and internal enemies)
And those who strive for Us—We will surely guide them to Our ways. And indeed, Allah is with the doers of good.

Qur'an, 11:118 (Diversity of human belief)
And if your Lord had willed, He could have made mankind one community; but they will not cease to differ.

Qur'an, 24:30–31 (Dress code and modesty)
Tell the believing men to reduce [some] of their vision and guard their private parts. That is purer for them. Indeed, Allah is acquainted with what they do. And tell the believing women to reduce [some] of their vision and guard their private parts and not expose their adornment except that which [necessarily]

appears thereof and to wrap [a portion of] their head coverings over their chests and not expose their adornment except to their husbands, their fathers, their husbands' fathers, their sons, their husbands' sons, their brothers, their brothers' sons, their sisters' sons, their women, that which their right hands possess, or those male attendants having no physical desire, or children who are not yet aware of the private aspects of women. And let them not stamp their feet to make known what they conceal of their adornment. And turn to Allah in repentance, all of you, O believers, that you might succeed.

Qur'an, 5:32 (Value of human life)
Because of that, We decreed upon the Children of Israel that whoever kills a soul unless for a soul or for corruption [done] in the land—it is as if he had slain mankind entirely. And whoever saves one—it is as if he had saved mankind entirely. And our messengers had certainly come to them with clear proof. Then indeed many of them, [even] after that, throughout the land, were transgressors.

Qur'an, 31: 14–15 (Relationship with non-Muslim parents)
And We have enjoined upon man [care] for his parents. His mother carried him, [increasing her] in weakness upon weakness, and his weaning is in two years. Be grateful to Me and to your parents; to Me is the [final] destination. But if they endeavor to make you associate with Me that of which you have no knowledge, do not obey them but accompany them in [this] world with appropriate kindness and follow the way of those who turn back to Me [in repentance]. Then to Me will be your return, and I will inform you about what you used to do.

Qur'an, 30:2-4 (Prediction in the Qur'an)

The Byzantines have been defeated in the nearest land. But they, after their defeat, will overcome within three to nine years. To Allah belongs the command before and after. And that day the believers will rejoice.

Qur'an, 17:70 (Human dignity and honor)

And We have certainly honored the children of Adam and carried them on the land and sea and provided for them of the good things and preferred them over much of what We have created, with [definite] preference.

Qur'an, 16:90 (Allah orders to observe and support justice)

Indeed, Allah orders justice and good conduct and giving to relatives and forbids immorality and bad conduct and oppression. He admonishes you that perhaps you will be reminded.

Qur'an, 49:13 (Equality)

O mankind, indeed We have created you from male and female and made you peoples and tribes that you may know one another. Indeed, the most noble of you in the sight of Allah is the most righteous of you. Indeed, Allah is Knowing and Acquainted.

A Brief Glossary of Islamic Terms

This list is courtesy of GainPeace.org

AL-HAMDULILLAH: "All praise be to Allah."

ALLAH: The proper name of the Creator of the universe, i.e. God.

ASR: Late afternoon ritual prayer.

AYAH: A verse of the Holy Qur'an (also means a "sign" of God).

BISMILLAH: "In the Name of Allah.," This statement is made by Muslims before a lawful endeavor.

DEEN: Usually translated as "religion." Deen is a comprehensive way of life.

DUA: Supplication, or personal prayer.

EID AL-FITR: Festival marking the end of Ramadan, the ninth month of the Islamic lunar calendar.

EID AL-ADHA: The Feast of Sacrifice, which starts on the tenth day of the twelfth month of the Islamic lunar calendar. Hajj is also performed in the same month.

FAJR: Name of the first prayer of the day, performed before sunrise. There are five daily obligatory prayers.

FATIHA: The opening Surah (chapter) of the Qur'an; Fatiha is recited in every prayer.

HADITH: Sayings and traditions of Prophet Muhammad (peace be upon him).

HAJJ: Pilgrimage to the holy city of Mecca. Hajj is to be performed at least once in a lifetime. Hajj is performed in the twelfth month of the Islamic lunar calendar.

HIJAB: Veil worn by Muslim women for reasons of modesty and protection as commanded by God.

IMAM: Leader. A person who leads the prayer; can also be used for a Muslim scholar.

IMAN: Faith.

'ISA: Arabic word for Jesus Christ. Islam regards Jesus as a mighty Prophet of God, but not as the Son of God.

ISHA: Night Prayer. Last prayer of the day. There are five daily obligatory prayers.

ISLAM: Literally means "submission" to the will of Allah and peace that comes with this submission.

JAHANNAM: Hell.

JANNAH: Paradise.

JIBREEL: (Archangel ?)Gabriel.

JIHAD: To struggle one's utmost to be a better person in the sight of Allah. Does not exclusively denote armed conflict.

JUMMAH: "Friday," the Muslim's day of gathering for Friday early afternoon prayers.

KA'BAH: The first and holiest shrine constructed for the worship of One God, found in Mecca (Makkah), Saudi Arabia. Rebuilt by Prophet Abraham and Ishmael.

KAFIR: Unbeliever, who has rejected the truth of Islam.

KHALIFA: A Muslim ruler of an Islamic State.

KHUTBA: Sermon. Usually refers to the Friday sermon.

MAGHRIB: Sunset Prayer. Fourth prayer of five daily prayers.

MALA'IKAH: Angels.

MASJID: Mosque, place of worship for Muslims.

MUHAMMAD: The name of the final Messenger and Prophet of God to humanity. Muslims say, "Peace be upon him," after saying his name in order to honor and show respect for the Prophet.

MUHARRAM: The first month of the Islamic calendar.

MUSLIM: Follower of Islam. Literally means "The one who submits" (i.e. To the will of Allah).

QIBLA: Direction in which all Muslims face when praying, which is the Ka'bah in Mecca, Saudi Arabia. The direction is generally northeast in USA.

QUR'AN: Scripture of Muslims. The last revelation of Allah given to humanity, through His last Prophet and Messenger, Muhammad (peace be upon him).

RAMADAN: The month of Fasting, the ninth month of the Islamic lunar calendar.

SAHABI: Companion of Prophet Muhammad (peace be upon him).

SAJDA: Prostration, as in prayer.

SALAAM: Peace. Muslims greet each other by saying "As-Salaamu alaykum"—peace be upon you. The response to this is "Wa alaykum as-Salam" —peace be upon you too!

SALAAT: Prayer. Muslims pray five times a day.

SALLALLAHU ALAIHE WA SALLAM: "May the peace and blessings of Allah be upon him." This phrase is recited whenever the name of the Prophet Muhammad (peace and blessing of Allah be upon him) is mentioned.

SHAHADAH: The creed of Islam: "I bear witness that there is no deity worthy of worship except Allah, and I bear witness that Muhammad is the Messenger of Allah." The way for a person to formally embrace Islam is to consciously recite the "Shahadah" and fully believe in it. It is the first of the five pillars of Islam.

SHAITAN: Satan. Satan is not a fallen angel according to Islam, but a different creation (i.e. Jinn).

SHARI'AH: Islamic Law. It encompasses both the Qur'an and Hadith, the sayings of the Prophet Muhammad (peace be upon him). Shari'ah provides guidance to an individual Muslims and to an Islamic state.

SHIRK: Associating partners with Allah. The grave sin of shirk is not forgiven if a person dies in that state.

SUBHAN ALLAH: "Glory be to Allah."

SUBHANA WA TA'LA: Sometimes abbreviated as "swt," which means "The Glorified and Exalted." Muslims customarily utter this after taking the name of Allah.

SURAH: Chapter of the Qur'an. The Qur'an has 114 Surahs (chapters).

TAHARA: Purification of the body, clothing, and the soul.

TAWHEED: The Divine Unity, in its most profound sense. Allah is One in His Essence and His Attributes and His Acts.

UMRA: The lesser pilgrimage to Mecca, but not during the Hajj period.

WUDU: Purification with water before performing prayers.

ZAKAT: Obligatory charity. One of the five pillars of Islam.

ZUHR: Also spelled "Dhuhr." Early afternoon prayer, the second prayer of the five daily prayers.

References and Further Reading

Translation of The Qur'an (Oxford World's Classics) Paperback – June 15, 2008 by M. A. S. Abdel Haleem.

The Global Messenger (Mercy for the Worlds) – 2011 Compiled by Umm Muhammad Revised by: Osama Emara http://d1.islamhouse.com/data/en/ih_books/single/en_The_Global_Messenger.pdf

Armstrong, Karen. Muhammad: A Prophet for Our Time Paperback – August 28, 2007

Ramadan, Tariq. In the Footsteps of the Prophet: Lessons from the Life of Muhammad

Lings, Martin. Muhammad: His Life Based on the Earliest Sources Paperback – October 6, 2006

Lings, Martin. A Sufi Saint of the Twentieth Century: Shaikh Ahmad al-Alawi: His Spiritual Heritage and Legacy. Berkeley: University of California Press, 1971.

Mattson, Ingrid. The Story of the Qur'an: Its History and Place in Muslim Life. Malden, MA: Blackwell Pub., 2013.

Esack, Farid. On Being a Muslim: Finding a Religious Path in the World Today. Oxford: Oneworld, 1999.

Nasr, Seyyed H. A Young Muslim's Guide to the Modern World. South Elgin, IL: Library of Islam, 1994.

Hanson, Hamza Yusuf. "The Sunna: The Way of The Prophet Muhammad," in Voices Of Islam, ed. Vincent Cornell Vol. 1. Westport: Praeger, 2006.

Jalal, al-Din Rumi, trans. John Moyne, and Coleman Barks. Open Secret: Versions of Rumi. Boston: Shambhala, 1999.

Silverstein, Adam J. Islamic History: A Very Short Introduction. Oxford University Press, 2010.

Karim, Jamillah and Dawn-Marie Gibson. "Women of the Nation: Between Black Protest and Sunni Islam," NYU Press. July 2014.

Gardel, Mattias. "In the Name of Elijah Muhammad: Louis Farrakhan and The Nation of Islam." Duke University Press. 1996.

Esposito, John L. Islam: The Straight Path. New York: Oxford University Press, 1998.

Reese, Scott S. "Islam in Africa / Africans in Islam," in The Journal of African History 55:1, March 2014.

Levi, Scott. "Turks and Tajiks in Central Asian History," in Sahadeo, Jeff and Russell G. Zanca. Everyday Life in Central Asia: Past and Present. Bloomington: Indiana University Press, 2007.

Levi, Scott C., and Ron Sela. "Islamic Central Asia: An Anthology of Historical Sources." Bloomington: Indiana University Press, 2009.

Menocal, Maria R. The Ornament of the World: How Muslims, Jews, and Christians Created a Culture of Tolerance in Medieval Spain. Boston: Back Bay Books / Little, Brown and Company, 2002.

Metcalf, Barbara D. Islam in South Asia in Practice. Princeton University Press, 2009.

Quataert, Donald. The Ottoman Empire, 1700–1922. New York: Cambridge University Press, 2000.

Fox, James J., ed., Religion and Ritual, Indonesian Heritage series, Vol. 9, Singapore: Didier Millet, 1998.

Pringle, Robert. Understanding Islam in Indonesia: Politics and Diversity. Honolulu: Hawaii University Press, 2010.

Saliba, George. "Islamic Science and the Making of the European Renaissance (Transformations: Studies in the History of Science and Technology)." MIT Press, 2011.

Smith, Jane I. Islam in America. New York: Columbia University Press, 1999.

الحمد لله رب العالمين

"All Praise and Gratitude is due to Allah,
Lord of the Worlds..."